Gien Karssen is a sto... studies about the wor... ...ave never read one more practical than *Her Name Is Woman*. Gien makes these biblical women really come alive as you observe their actions and the effects of their lives. She helps you draw out applications which are relevant today. Gien is one of the best trainers I know for young Bible study leaders. She brings the Word of God to bear upon situations in day-to-day living. My prayer is that this book will work as a seed that brings forth much fruit.

CORRIE TEN BOOM
Author of *The Hiding Place*

All my life I have read about the women of the Bible, learning much from them even though they were somewhat vague, historic characters. In this book, these same characters have suddenly come alive. Because of Gien's careful research, sanctified imagination, and skill as a writer, I found myself understanding these women and their situations in a new way. Knowing more about the customs of their day helps us understand better why they acted as they did. It is interesting to note that God's women, down through the centuries, have enjoyed a freedom the world will find difficult to understand— the freedom to be and to do that which God intended. You will find this book both interesting and enlightening.

RUTH BELL GRAHAM
Author of *Footprints of a Pilgrim*

Leaders

lessons from women of vision and courage

HER NAME IS WOMAN BIBLE STUDY

Gien Karssen

NavPress

A NavPress resource published in alliance
with Tyndale House Publishers, Inc.

NavPress is the publishing ministry of The Navigators, an international Christian organization and leader in personal spiritual development. NavPress is committed to helping people grow spiritually and enjoy lives of meaning and hope through personal and group resources that are biblically rooted, culturally relevant, and highy practical.

For more information, visit www.NavPress.com.

Leaders: Lessons from Women of Vision and Courage

Copyright © 1975, 1977, 2015 by Stichting Manninne. All rights reserved.

A NavPress resource published in alliance with Tyndale House Publishers, Inc.

NAVPRESS is a registered trademark of NavPress, The Navigators, Colorado Springs, CO. The NAVPRESS logo is a trademark of NavPress, The Navigators. *TYNDALE* is a registered trademark of Tyndale House Publishers, Inc. Absence of * in connection with marks of NavPress or other parties does not indicate an absence of registration of those marks.

The Team:

Don Pape, Publisher

Caitlyn Carlson, Acquisitions Editor

Cover design by Jacqueline L. Nuñez

Cover photograph of woman copyright © Digital Vision/Getty Images. All rights reserved.

Cover illustration of wreath copyright © MarushaBelle/Shutterstock. All rights reserved.

For information about special discounts for bulk purchases, please contact Tyndale House Publishers at csresponse@tyndale.com, or call 1-800-323-9400.

Library of Congress Cataloging-in-Publication Data

Karssen, Gien.

   Her name is woman : leaders : lessons from women of vision and courage / Gien Karssen.

     pages cm

    ISBN 978-1-63146-416-4

1. Women in the Bible—Biography.   2. Bible—Biography.   3. Leadership in the Bible.

4. Leadership—Biblical teaching.   I. Title.

    BS575.K36932 2015

    220.9'2082—dc23   2015012233

Printed in the United States of America

24	23	22	21	20	19	18
8	7	6	5	4	3	2

I dedicate this book to my many friends within The Navigators organization around the world. The plan to write the Her Name Is Woman series began to ripen through my global contact with young women. I saw in them the same fascination for the lives of women in the Bible that I have.

I further remember many, many others, men and women, who through their teachings, example, and friendship have made an indelible impression upon my life. I think of the first Navigator I met years ago, Dawson Trotman, the founder of the organization, and of the many young people who have found a personal faith in Jesus Christ through the ministry of The Navigators recently.

They all have three things in common: a great love for God, a deep reverence for His Word, and a passion to share their lives with others. Two words are applicable to almost all of them: realism and enthusiasm.

Through my fellowship with The Navigators, the intense desire to be a woman after the heart of God grew within me. For this reason the women in this book are not just people of a dim, distant past, but real people, living and sparkling. It is my desire that every person who reads this book will be challenged in the same way to live wholeheartedly for God. It is my desire that they be encouraged and built up. And, at the same time, I trust this book will prove to be an instrument in their hands whereby they can help others.

Contents

Contents

Foreword

As a little girl, I dreamed grand dreams. Whether it was to be a princess in a castle, president of the United States, a famous actress, or a corporate CEO, I wanted to believe I could do something great.

We all long for a life of significance. We want to matter. We hope we can make a difference. For those of us with leadership gifts, the desire for influence can be consuming.

We quickly identify heroes and role models. We look for others to guide the way—to help us make sense of our gifts and longings. We're eager to learn and grow.

Every aspiring leader needs an example to follow, and Gien Karssen has given us the examples we crave. In this book, Gien brings to life the stories of amazing women leaders from Scripture. Providing historical and cultural background, she sets the stage for us to understand the particulars of their stories. She helps us find parts of ourselves in their strengths and weaknesses. She provides portraits of strength and humility to which we can aspire.

I encourage you to read this book slowly and contemplatively. Imagine yourself in each woman's context. Consider how you may have reacted in her circumstances. See where her strengths and her sin collided, and ask God to give you wisdom for how her leadership story applies to yours. Ponder the questions carefully. What might God be saying to you?

There is no greater place for us to seek leadership wisdom than the pages of Scripture. Gien's work reminds us that God didn't neglect to leave us examples of great women who have gone before us.

May their stories inspire you and draw out your greatest leadership!

Jenni Catron, church leader and author of Clout

How to Use This Study

Do you long for a meaningful life? Do you want to become whole and fulfilled? These inborn, inner urges originate from the commission God gave woman at her creation. He expects woman, an equal partner with man, to be willing to step into her calling. The spiritual side of a woman is extremely important.

The women in this book are not fictional. They are real. They lived in history and, in their desires and problems, in their hopes and ambitions, are living among us today. Though the Bible doesn't share the full extent of their stories, I imaginatively explore what these women may have been doing and feeling in the time and place in which God placed them, in hopes that you will connect with their journeys even further.

As you learn about each of the women throughout the Her Name Is Woman series, the central question you must ask is, What place does God have in her life? The answer to this question decides the extent of every woman's happiness, usefulness, and motivation to keep moving forward. If God is absent, or if He is not given His rightful place, then life is without true purpose—without perspective.

As you read this book, join with these women of the Bible to consider your attitude toward God. And I hope that as you get acquainted with these women, you will make a fresh or renewed start in getting to know the Word of God.

I trust that meeting these women will turn out to be an unexpected gift for you and that you will resonate deeply with their experiences—and I pray that they will show you the way to a richer and happier life with God and other people.

AS YOU BEGIN

You may approach this book in one of two ways. First, just read it. The stories are intended to draw you deeply into the life of each woman in these pages. But be sure to include the Bible passages referenced at the beginning of each chapter in your reading. They are an important part of the book and are necessary for understanding the chapter. Second, you may wish to discuss the book in a small group. Considering the subjects and questions with some other people will add depth and greater insight to your study of these women.

Scripture references at the bottom of many pages will help you dig deeper into the Bible's wealth of truth and wisdom. You may answer the questions throughout each chapter personally or discuss them with your group. You may also conduct topical studies of these women or research accompanying themes. Whatever your direction might be, this study will become richer as you discuss these women with others, especially after your own individual preparation. Whether you do this study on your own or with others, be sure to use a journal so you may record your thoughts on the questions and any other things God impresses on your heart through the course of this study.

SUGGESTIONS FOR BIBLE STUDY GROUPS

1. Start with a small group—usually with a minimum of six and a maximum of ten people. This way your group will be large enough for an interesting discussion, but small enough for each member to participate. As your number increases, start a second group.

2. Before you start the group, decide how often you want to meet. Many people may hesitate to give themselves to something new for an indefinite period of time. There are twelve chapters in each book of the Her Name Is Woman series, so they may easily be used as twelve-week studies. However, these books can just as easily work as six-week studies (two chapters per week). Some chapters are longer and will take more time to work through, while others are short enough to be combined into a two-part lesson. Please note that the number of questions varies depending on the length of the lesson. Discuss what process will work best for your group.

3. Remember that a Bible study group should discuss the Bible. While many of the questions within this book

are designed to help women examine their individual faith journeys, Scripture informs every piece of the study and should be referenced as an integral part of the discussion. Each participant should prepare her study at home beforehand so each member may share her personal findings.

4. Stress the necessity of applying the lessons learned, and help one another in doing this. There is a far greater need for spiritual growth than for an increase of knowledge. "How can what I learned influence my life?" is a question each participant should ask herself.

5. Determine, before you start, to attend every meeting. Miss only when you absolutely cannot attend. If you can't attend, do the study anyway and make up for it at the next meeting.

6. Consider yourself a member of the group. Feel free to make a contribution. Lack of experience should not keep you from taking part in the discussion. On the other hand, resist the temptation to dominate the group.

SUGGESTIONS FOR LEADERS OF BIBLE STUDY GROUPS

- Be sure that you have given sufficient time to your own Bible study and that you have completed it.
- Come prepared. Make notes of the points you want to stress.

- Begin and end on time. Set the tone by starting promptly at the first meeting.
- Few mountain climbers enjoy being carried to the top. Leave the joy of climbing to the group members. Don't do all the talking. Guide the discussion in such a way that each member of the group can participate.
- Don't allow any one person to dominate the conversation. Gently guide women so each person may have an opportunity to speak. Sometimes it is necessary to talk privately with the overtalkative person, explaining the necessity of group participation. While some women may prefer to remain quiet, give them the opportunity to participate by asking them specific questions.
- Use the questions throughout each chapter as a jumping-off point, but feel the freedom to focus on issues that seem to particularly resonate with your group. However, don't allow the group to get too off topic. If a particular question becomes too time consuming or detracts from the overall study, redirect the conversation back to the main study. Getting back on track when the subject begins to wander can be done by saying, "Perhaps we could discuss this further after the study," or "Let's return to the main focus of the study."
- At the beginning of each session, open with prayer. Pray that Christ will speak to each person present by His Word. At the end of each session, pray for yourself and for each member of the group. Pray that the Holy Spirit will make you sensitive to the needs of others.

A NOTE BEFORE

You may be tempted to think that many of the women in this study have nothing to teach you. *I am not a leader*, you may say. You may think you are too quiet, or too shy, or not influential. But as you look at the lives of each of these women, be encouraged. Leadership is not always a role that is bestowed. God-centered leadership is first and foremost a heart attitude. You may lead through your attitude in your home, or through your advice in your friendships, or through your service in your church. You are a leader if through your submission to God you offer guidance and perspective to those around you. As you step into the lives of these women—who range from outspoken prophetesses to servant-hearted stay-at-home mothers—be encouraged that God has equipped you to lead exactly where you are.

1

MIRIAM

A Leader Who Overestimated Herself

Search me, O God, and know my heart; test my thoughts.
Point out anything you find in me that makes you sad, and
lead me along the path of everlasting life.

PSALM 139:23-24, TLB

READ

Exodus 15:19-21; Numbers 12:1-15; Numbers 20:1

• • •

MIRIAM HAD BEEN AN INTELLIGENT CHILD. Her mother had
readily entrusted her with an assignment of such importance
that the life of her youngest brother was dependent upon her
success. She completed her task with courage and tact, bringing her mother, a Hebrew woman, and an Egyptian princess
in contact with one another. Thus her brother was rescued,
benefiting both their family and God's people.[1] The child
was Moses, mediator of the old covenant, the prophet who
spoke face-to-face with God.

---
[1] Exodus 2:1-10

As an adult, Miriam was a woman of stature. Her character had been formed in a family where faith was a daily reality. Her parents had the courage, the love, and the ingenuity to defy the commands of a tyrannical king in order to save the life of their youngest son. The family of Amram and Jochebed was unique in Israel's existence, for it brought forth three great leaders—Moses, Aaron, and Miriam—who all served the nation at the same time.

"I brought you up out of Egypt and redeemed you from the land of slavery. I sent Moses to lead you, also Aaron and Miriam," God later declared through the prophet Micah.[2] When Moses led his troublesome people out of Egypt to Canaan, he was assisted by his brother Aaron, the high priest, and his sister Miriam, the prophetess.

She was not just a tagalong sister. She was his colaborer, with leadership responsibilities. God called Miriam, an unmarried woman, to an exceptional task. She had the privilege of being the first female prophet—a spokeswoman for God.

In deeds and words she proclaimed the greatness of God. Her life was totally centered on loving God and His people. Her gifts and interests were too great to be used exclusively for the small family circle. Israel had many wives and mothers, but only one Miriam. God entrusted her with a high position. An entire nation was dependent upon her. She received supreme satisfaction in life, as she dedicated herself wholly to the task.

[2] Micah 6:4

What gifts has God entrusted you with? How are
you using those gifts? Are there any other ways
in which God is prompting you to use your gifts?

She was nearing the age of one hundred when the miracle of the Red Sea astounded the masses. The water that brought salvation to God's people confirmed the fall of His enemies. "I will sing to the LORD, for He has triumphed gloriously," cried Moses afterward. "He has hurled both horse and rider into the sea."[3] After the men had started the joyous singing, the women continued it. From that day forth, Israel would always sing about exceptional victories because of Miriam. She was first in line—energetic and youthful in spirit despite her age. With a timbrel in her hand, she took over the song from Moses. She encouraged the women to dance to the honor of God while shouting for joy: "Sing to the LORD, for he has triumphed gloriously."[4]

How do you praise God when He does great
things? Do you inspire others to praise as well?

Miriam was a born leader. The women readily followed her. And although they could not foresee the future, singing

---

[3] Exodus 15:1, NLT
[4] Exodus 15:20, NLT

would become an endless source of support to the women during their long wilderness wanderings. The journey was long because of the disobedience of the people, and it was going to be necessary to encourage one another with the faithfulness of God. They gained new courage when singing, "He has hurled both horse and rider into the sea."

But self-conceit was becoming fatal to Miriam.

She was a strong woman. Leadership came easily to her. And, as is often the case, this very strength became a weakness. It has been said that circumstances reveal the inner person. The circumstance that revealed Miriam's inner character was Moses' second marriage, this time to an Ethiopian.

———

In what ways do your strengths also act as weaknesses? How has God led you to combat those weaknesses?

———

It is understandable that Miriam found this difficult. It was strange that Moses, a man of God, would again marry a woman from another nation. Or was Miriam simply reacting to the presence of another woman in the life of Moses, especially since she was unmarried herself? Was she indignant because he was satisfied with a foreign woman, while countless Israelite women would have been more suitable? These questions are not answered in the Scriptures.

Moses, the great leader of the Israelites, was Miriam's youngest brother, and she was worried about him. She was concerned about how the results of this marriage might affect the people. The marriage took place in a period of history when relatives usually decided upon matters of marriage. Looking at her concern from this standpoint, it would seem to be a proper spiritual reaction from a mature woman. But it was far from that.

Miriam, who had ascended to the highest post ever held by a woman, and who was named by God in the same breath as the two great male leaders, had simply surpassed her boundaries. She overestimated herself. She considered herself to be on the same level as Moses. And in her pride she undermined his authority. "Is he, indeed, the leader of the three of us?" she asked. "Are not Aaron and I his equals?"[5]

How do you react when an authority figure makes a decision you disagree with? When God does or allows something you disagree with, in what ways, if any, does your response differ?

Miriam was not motivated by concern for the well-being of the people or for Moses, but by jealousy. Aaron, the most pliable of the three, could not resist his domineering sister, so he went along with her. Together Miriam and Aaron tried to usurp Moses' authority. In doing this, they endangered the unity and future of the entire nation. Moreover, they attempted to thwart the direct revelation of God. Instead of

[5] Numbers 12:12, author's paraphrase

thinking about the well-being of everyone concerned, they thought only selfishly.[6]

Have you ever used your influence out of poor motives? How did God correct you in that time?

God created humans to give themselves to others. When we do this, we experience the greatest happiness. It enriches and widens our horizons. But our lives become poor and limited when we selfishly desire only to receive—when our self is in the center of our thinking.

Moses remained calm. He showed no desire to defend himself. There was, however, another who defended Moses' rights, and this became a frightful experience for Miriam and Aaron. For God in heaven heard, knew, and saw what was happening on earth. He took immediate steps to stop the rebellion against Moses' leadership and to punish the guilty ones.

Shattered and with shaky knees, Aaron and Miriam appeared before God. They heard how He judged the situation. Moses, they heard, was not only the undisputed leader; he was also given a position higher than all the prophets.

It was clear that God had chosen Moses to be the mediator between Himself and His people. He respected Moses so highly that He didn't speak to him through vague riddles and obscure dreams. Instead, He spoke to Moses as a man speaks to his friends[7]—openly, plainly.

[6] Philippians 2:3-4
[7] Exodus 33:11

Miriam and Aaron had attacked a man highly respected by God. When He in His godly justice and authority called them to account, they had no excuse. Ultimately they had not harmed Moses, but themselves. Moses, the God-appointed mediator, was a foreshadowing of the Savior to come. To reject Moses was, in fact, to reject the Messiah. This was what made the situation so serious.

_____

Do you respect the leaders God has appointed in your church? If so, how do you communicate that respect? If not, are your reasons biblically based, or are they subjective?

_____

When God left them in His anger, Miriam became a leper. Leprosy was the most dreaded of diseases, for it sapped the strength of the person who had it, degrading her with a walking death. And God had stained Miriam with the curse of leprosy.

The woman who for years had gone ahead of the crowd singing, who had challenged the other women to sing praises to God, had been expelled from the ranks of leadership. Her voice, which had once so melodiously praised God, now shouted a hoarse "unclean, unclean," when anyone came within her reach. The members of her body would gradually become more and more hideous, until they finally dropped off. She would go through life crippled and lonely until her death.

Miriam had to experience very painfully how great her sin was in the eyes of God. The shame of her deed could be compared to a father spitting in the face of his child publicly. Therefore, she had to undergo her punishment publicly, so that everyone could see how God punished people who thought too highly of themselves.[8] Miriam, the brave, active woman, found no words to answer His curse.

Do you view disrespect of leadership as sin?
If so, how does this inform your response
when leaders make decisions you don't like?

Aaron regained his composure first and indicated that he had accepted the correction. He said to Moses, "Oh, my lord"—he did not call him "brother," but "lord," thus recognizing Moses' leadership. "Don't punish us for being foolish and sinning."[9] Aaron identified himself completely with Miriam's sin. Then it was not he, the high priest, but Moses who entreated God for her healing. Moses didn't indicate that he approved of God's judgment, nor did he rebuke Miriam and Aaron. He simply prayed to God, and his prayer reduced Miriam's sentence from one of lifelong suffering to only seven days.

Miriam's attitude had brought harm not only to herself but also to her people. Their journey had been delayed because

[8] Romans 12:3
[9] Numbers 12:11, author's paraphrase

of her sin. The entire nation was kept from moving forward until Miriam was among them again. The seven days she spent as an outcast must have given Miriam much food for thought. Did she then understand that God Himself appoints His leaders? That in His godly order He entrusts leadership to those who are humble enough to be willing to serve?[10] Had she come out a better person? Had she been purified?

Have you ever observed someone create discord within your church body due to lack of respect for leadership? How was the issue resolved? Were there any long-term effects of the discord?

The Bible doesn't record any further rebellion. Had the experience destroyed Miriam's strength and usefulness? Did she lose her gift of prophecy? The Bible doesn't say, but it does state that she died before her people entered the Promised Land.

What do Philippians 2:3-4 and Romans 12:3 teach about criticism and overestimating oneself?

Miriam was a woman at the top. It was an exceptional position, a commission that had been entrusted to her by

[10] Luke 22:24-27; 1 Peter 5:5-6

God. Miriam's story offered a wonderful example as long as she used her position to honor God. A person who does this can hardly go wrong. However, Miriam gradually shifted away from accepting God's control in her life to trying to control things herself. This no doubt occurred so subtly that she didn't realize the change was taking place. Perhaps if she had searched her heart honestly in time, she could have prevented God's judgment.[11] Perhaps then she would not have overstepped her boundaries by overestimating herself.

---

*Take an honest assessment of your life.
Do your actions show a reliance on God's
control, or your own? How might you model
your life off of the positive example Miriam
set in her early leadership and avoid the
negative example of her later years?*

---

[11] 1 Corinthians 11:31

2
DEBORAH

A Leader of a Nation Who Was Inspired by Faith

God is looking for people to use, and if you can get usable,
he will wear you out. The most dangerous prayer you can
pray is this: "Use me."

RICK WARREN

READ

Judges 4–5

• • •

THE SITUATION IN ISRAEL was gloomy and desolate. Life
had become nearly unbearable and unsettled. All trade was
paralyzed as caravans stopped traveling through the valley
of Jezreel to the south or east. Farming was limited to the
minimum. Hardly a farmer dared to till his ground for fear
of being killed during a surprise enemy attack.

With traffic at a standstill, the streets were deserted. The
inhabitants of the mountain villages moved outside their
homes a little more often than the others, but they still preferred to use the narrow side paths.

For more than twenty years the land had been occupied,
and the conquerors had kept the people firmly under their

thumbs. Young people knew the word *freedom* only from the mouths of their parents. For the older people, it was getting increasingly difficult to remember what that word really meant. The population was downhearted, fearful, and depressed.

King Jabin, who lived in the northern city of Hazor, dominated all of Israel. His dreaded right-hand man, General Sisera, commanded a large army that had nine hundred chariots.[1] Everyone was afraid of him, for his forces could overrun and trample down the countryside swiftly and with deadly intent. Only the mountain people were relatively safe, for his chariots could not reach them.

The cause of this misery, however, did not lie with the occupation forces but with the Israelite people themselves. After eighty years of prosperity under the previous rulers, Judges Ehud and Shamgar, the Israelites had shown no gratitude toward God. They fell away from Him and started to worship idols.

The results of their actions were predictable. The people who thought that they no longer needed God now had to experience His distance.[2] When He withdrew His protection, they became powerless against their enemies, and peace disappeared.

Yet not all of the roads in the country were deserted. In the hill country of Ephraim, on the road between Bethel and Ramah, more and more people were going to a palm tree that stood plainly above the surrounding shrubbery. Under that tree, their present leader—the prophetess Deborah—held

[1] Judges 4:3
[2] Judges 4:2

court, judged the people, and gave direction to their lives.[3] She was the only female judge among the twelve judges who ruled between the times of Joshua and Samuel.

She held a twofold position among her people. She was both their national and spiritual leader and carried out her duties capably and with good results. Like so many times before in their tumultuous history, distress was causing the Israelites to seek God. In this situation, Deborah had the privilege of being His instrument. Because of her faith, the events that happened changed history.

Deborah's responsibilities were those of a man in that time period. She hadn't arrived at her position by subduing a man, however, and had not appropriated power illegally. God had given her those responsibilities. She had been appointed to bring the people back to God, to liberate them from the power of their oppressors. The entire nation acknowledged her as its leader. Therefore, as Deborah judged in spiritual and material affairs, she also instructed her people in the things of God.

In areas within your life in which you act as a leader—whether at work, in the home, at church, or in your friendships—do you lead out of a sense of entitlement or a desire to control? How do you seek God's leading and recognize His role in giving you that place of leadership?

---

[3] Judges 4:4-5

She was the wife of Lappidoth, who assumed a minor role. In the events that were to follow, she would be the principal leader. Among the people of her time—men and women alike—she was as exceptional as the palm tree in her land that was later named after her. She was outstanding and unique.

Deborah thought and made her decisions based on her walk with God. Her leadership had form and content. She performed her tasks brilliantly, intelligently, and with self-sacrificial perseverance.

She was the mediator between God and His people, the proclaimer of His Word. In her high position, she communicated insight, wisdom, and the knowledge of God with love to her people. With the fine-tuned intuition of a person who abides in the presence of God, she sensed that God's time had come to throw off the yoke of oppression.

In what situations and relationships has God positioned you to share wisdom? How does your relationship with Him inform your attitude in those situations?

"Those who are wise will find a time and a way to do what is right," wrote Solomon.[4] Deborah proved that statement correct. She not only discerned the time of God's action in the history of her people but also received insight into the very method He wanted to use to liberate them.

---
[4] Ecclesiastes 8:5, NLT

She felt that as a woman she was not the appointed person to fight this war. So the command went out to Barak, the son of Abinoam of Kedesh: "Mobilize 10,000 men."[5]

For years as God's messenger, she had worked toward freedom and prayed for it. But now that the time had come for it to be realized, someone else was to put God's commands into action. With wisdom and tact, Deborah found the right way to approach Barak.

Think of a situation in which you had to take the back seat because God had better equipped someone else to complete the task. Was your heart open to God's leading in this situation, or did you struggle to relinquish control?

She understood that all human authority was, in fact, delegated authority. The only one who had real and final authority was God. So although she was first among her people, Deborah did not place herself over Barak. Instead she placed herself next to him and together with him placed herself under God's leadership. As she walked with God, she lost the desire to hold all the glory. Other people became more important to her. She executed leadership by inspiring others.

---
[5] Judges 4:6, author's paraphrase

---

*Submission to God's leadership gives us
the ability to take whatever place He asks
of us—whether it is one of leadership,
teamwork, or submission to others. Which
of these roles is hardest for you? How might
you cultivate your attitude of submission
to God in order to grow in this area?*

She derived her motivation from the God of Israel. Never, not even for a single moment, did she doubt that the Almighty One—who had rescued His people out of their problems in the past—would help them again.

Her command to Barak was at the same time an encouragement. "Don't be afraid because of their number," she said confidently. "Looking at it from God's point of view—our enemy is defeated already. The chariots and the forces of Jabin are nothing in the sight of God. The only thing He expects from you is faith."[6] In a couple of sentences, she placed the situation in its proper perspective.

Deborah's tactful, spiritual leadership had a freeing effect on Barak. It kept him from showing himself to be stronger than he was. He dared to accept the challenge, but not without Deborah. He was certain that God would be fighting for his forces only if she accompanied him. He acknowledged her as his superior in faith and courage. Yet because of these

---
[6] Judges 4:6-7, author's paraphrase

experiences, he developed into a man who is named among the heroes of faith in Hebrews 11.[7] He became a strong leader in the coming war.

Who in your life has provided spiritual leadership that challenged you into deeper faith?

Although Deborah's approach helped Barak become a hero for God, neither of them allowed thoughts of rancor or competition to come between them. They functioned in God's plan as instruments. Together as two people—a woman and a man[8]—they carried out God's orders. Each gave in voluntarily to the other for the well-being of the entire nation. They also knew that part of God's plan included their deliverance through a woman, Jael, the wife of Heber.[9]

Deborah and Barak functioned as one unit. Mutually they helped and completed each other. Together they moved from Ephraim to Kedesh, which was not far from where Jabin lived. There Barak recruited his soldiers. At the head of the newly formed army, Barak and Deborah climbed up the side of Mount Tabor together and looked down across the plains of Jezreel to their enemy camped at the foot of the mountain.

Throughout her constant cooperation with Barak, Deborah had remained the leader and the person responsible for all decisions. When the day to fight had come, God revealed His

[7] Hebrews 11:32-33
[8] Genesis 1:26-28
[9] Judges 4:9

will through her. "Arise!" she said to Barak. "For this is the day in which the LORD has given Sisera into your hands."[10] Again she followed up her command with encouragement. "Has not the Lord gone out before you? Don't be afraid of Sisera. This is not a fight between you and him but between him and God. The outcome of the battle is decided before it has begun. The victory is God's. He fights on your side."[11]

---

*How does knowing that God fights
for you impact your daily life?*

Deborah then watched as Barak, with his ten-thousand-man force behind him, stormed down the steep flank of Mount Tabor. Next to the Kishon River, he met Sisera's army arrayed behind the grim and armored chariots. The enemy expected an easy victory. Wasn't their opponent laughably small, an unworthy foe?

Had anyone looked toward the sky while the two armies were coming together? Gray thunderclouds moved together, rumbling ominously. Bad weather was at hand.

The storm broke in all its ferocity precisely at the moment the Israelites reached the plain. Heavy rain and hailstones beat into the faces of the enemy soldiers.[12] Before long the Kishon River overflowed its banks and became a wide stream. Wildly moving water churned the ground under the

---

[10] Judges 4:14, NASB
[11] Judges 4:14, author's paraphrase
[12] Flavius Josephus, *Antiquities of the Jews*, Book V, Chapter 5

warriors' feet into a muddy mess. The chariots of the enemy stuck fast, bringing defeat instead of victory. The routed enemy was unable to make a quick escape because of the pileup of chariots.

Barak and his men acknowledged God's hand in what was happening. They pursued the enemy with even more determination and killed every last man.[13] Sisera, seeing that all was lost, saw a chance to escape and ran for cover. But even he did not escape. He fell, like Deborah had predicted, by the hand of Jael.[14]

The occupation was over. Israel was free again. The oppression was gone. Normal living could finally take its course. Life had color and meaning again. The people had new goals; their future looked bright.

It is a known fact that it is hard for any person to stand up under adversity. Yet the character of someone is possibly even more tested when he or she is asked to execute power.

When have you gained insight into someone's character based on how he or she executed power? What implications does this have for your own life?

Since creation, God has decreed that a woman and a man—united through marriage—should carry out His commission

---

[13] Judges 4:16
[14] Judges 4:18-21

on earth. She was created as a partner with man, equal to him and yet different. Therefore she is suitable for him, capable of completing him.

This partnership between man and woman can reach complete fulfillment within marriage. But it can also take place in other contexts. Society has always functioned best when man and woman carried out their God-given tasks harmoniously. Deborah and Barak demonstrated that principle.

_____

What is one situation in your life in which you observe a partnership between a man and a woman working harmoniously? What is one situation in which you observe a breakdown in such a partnership? What do you think the difference is?

_____

Usually the man has been responsible for leadership. But in this passage, a woman was the leader. God does not always work according to a set pattern. He is looking for people who are willing to be used as instruments in any way He chooses.

Deborah didn't unduly execute her power. She simply lived up to her responsibilities. She was a fascinating and gifted woman who performed her varied tasks capably. A woman of enormous spiritual strength, she instructed her people in the laws of God. But she also turned around and gave skillful guidelines for a military operation. She knew how to use the sword as well as discernment.

Deborah's greatest strengths, however, were not her human capabilities, no matter how striking and many-sided they were. She knew that God had delegated strength and power to her. In everything she did, her expectation came from Him. Such people, written about in Isaiah,[15] continue to draw new strength over and over again despite their many exertions.

Deborah's victory song proved that her strength was in God. Her happiness was not, first and foremost, based on the deserved satisfaction of a task well done. Her deepest joy came from God.

"Listen, you kings! Pay attention, you mighty rulers! For I will sing to the LORD. I will make music to the LORD, the God of Israel," the song of Deborah and Barak began.[16] It ended with these words: "But let those who love Him be like the rising of the sun in its might."[17]

Deborah's life was strong and sparkling. Describing such a life, Solomon wrote, "But the path of the just is like the shining sun, that shines ever brighter unto the perfect day."[18]

Although God had first place in Deborah's epic song, she left a lot of room for others. Everyone who had a part in the victory—Barak, the leaders of the people, Jael—was elaborately mentioned.

Think of a recent victory in your life.
How might you honor God and others
for their role in that victory?

---

[15] Isaiah 40:31
[16] Judges 5:3, NLT
[17] Judges 5:31, NASB
[18] Proverbs 4:18, NKJV

Deborah did not claim honor for herself. Soberly she ascertained the fact that there were no leaders in Israel till she had arrived. How did she describe herself? She simply considered herself to be a mother in Israel. Just as a mother's attention is directed toward the well-being of her children, the deep desires of Deborah's heart were directed toward the welfare of her people.

Deborah is one of the outstanding women in biblical history because of her leadership, character, and beautiful poetry. Certainly she had a fascinating life. But her priorities were not based on her accomplishments. The open secret of her life was God. More than anything else, she showed what a woman can do when God is in complete control of her life. The possibilities are many-sided for a leader of a nation who wants to be inspired through faith in God.

3

ABIGAIL

A Woman Who Watched Over the Conscience of a Servant of God

A woman's inner beauty is almost always dependent upon her relationship with God.

EUGENIA PRICE, *THE UNIQUE WORLD OF WOMEN*

READ

1 Samuel 25

· · ·

HER HANDS MOVED QUICKLY.

Her thoughts ran even faster.

Although she realized that things were about to go very badly, Abigail did not panic or become nervous. Calmly she made her plans. She did not forget that she was pressed for time, that she could not lose one second.

The words of the servant a few moments ago kept resounding in her ears. "Know well what you have to do, madam," the servant had said, "for there is going to be great trouble ahead, for our master, for all of us. I am coming to you because

23

the boss is such a stubborn lout that no one can even talk to him."[1]

Because the situation was extremely serious[2] and there was no room for error, Abigail was handling everything herself. She didn't dare to leave such responsibilities to her servants.

She had to think quickly and accurately. What would six hundred ravenous men, living in the rough outdoors, need to still their hunger?

Abigail did not merely think of the most necessary essentials, such as bread and meat. She also packed roasted grain, raisins, delicious fig cakes, and wine.[3] She wanted to take good care of the men and bring them into a favorable mood.

Everything was taken care of quickly and efficiently. "Go on ahead," she ordered the servants. "I will follow you shorly."[4] Psychologically, it was a tactical move. Abigail's servants could start their work before she arrived.

She didn't talk to her husband, Nabal, about her plans, knowing that her words wouldn't penetrate his drunken stupor.

Nabal had arranged a great feast to celebrate his annual shearing of sheep. He was a wealthy man, possessing three thousand sheep and one thousand goats. The shearing of sheep was important, for wool was a vital commodity in the culture of Canaan.

After the extensive work was finished, Nabal offered the shearers—experts who were specially hired for this job— a meal. And the noisiest man at the table was Nabal himself.

[1] 1 Samuel 25:17, author's paraphrase
[2] 1 Samuel 25:1-22
[3] 1 Samuel 25:18
[4] 1 Samuel 25:19, NLT

Abigail's husband was the descendant of a great man, Caleb.[5] But he in no way resembled his illustrious forefather, who had excelled in insight, courage, and the fear of God. Nabal, whose name meant "the fool," was precisely that—a rude, clumsy fellow who failed to talk reasonably.

Look into your family history. What sort of spiritual legacy exists in your family? How are you reflecting or changing that legacy?

That was what David experienced when, through his messengers, he asked Nabal for food for himself and his six hundred followers. It was a normal request, for David and his men had formed a wall of protection around Nabal's sheep shearers to keep robbers and roving nomads from harming them during their work. Any Arab sheik—even today—could have asked for the same treatment and not have been rejected.

David had made his request modestly. His messengers had approached Nabal in a submissive manner just as David requested, like a son would to his father. Despite his tactful approach, Nabal's reaction was rude and insulting. "Who is this David?" he had snorted. "Who is this son of Jesse? Many servants are breaking away from their masters these days. Why should I take my bread and water, and the meat I have slaughtered for my shearers, and give it to men coming from who knows where?"[6]

---

[5] 1 Samuel 25:3; Numbers 14:6-10,24
[6] 1 Samuel 25:10-11

How do you respond when someone asks you to do something you don't want to do? What does your response indicate about what you value?

This answer was extremely offensive to David, who was popular throughout the entire country. Women from all the towns of Israel had been singing about his victories,[7] and he had already been anointed to be the next king. Even Nabal's servants praised him for his help and for the way he disciplined his men.[8] He had demonstrated prudent and strong leadership, keeping his soldiers organized and responsive to his commands.

Despite these factors, Nabal treated David like an insignificant man, a rebel whose requests he did not need to take into serious consideration.

David reacted to this scornful treatment with an outburst of rage. Only recently he had refused to avenge himself on Saul, who had tried to kill him, and had left the matter for God to judge.[9] During his fight with the insulting and cursing giant Goliath, he had thought only of the name of his God.[10] The man who later in history would be known as a man after God's heart[11] could not ignore this personal insult. He wanted to take immediate revenge.

---

[7] 1 Samuel 18:6-7
[8] 1 Samuel 25:15-16
[9] 1 Samuel 24:5-7
[10] 1 Samuel 17:45-47
[11] Acts 13:22

---

*Read 1 Samuel 24, 1 Samuel 17, and
2 Samuel 16:1-13. Why do you think David's
response in the situation with Nabel was
different from his responses in these passages?*

"Gird your sword, every one of you," he commanded. "No male in Nabal's house will remain alive. By tomorrow morning we will be finished with every one of them."[12] To avenge himself of Nabal's insult, David started on his way to the shepherd's home with four hundred men.

Abigail, meanwhile, mounted a donkey and rode to meet David. A woman who was humble enough to listen to the advice of a servant, she had enough character and courage to face David's anger. She was high-spirited, attractive, intelligent, and wise. Although the meaning of her name was "My Father [God] gives joy," it did not reflect her present circumstances, chained as she was by her marriage to Nabal. We can only vaguely guess what living with such a foolish brute had meant for such a believing and sensitive woman.

---

*Think of a difficult partnership you
have been in (with a coworker,
spouse, etc.). How did you reflect the
character of God in that situation?*

---

[12] 1 Samuel 25:13,22, author's paraphrase

This certainly was not the first time that Abigail had tried to glue together the pieces her husband had broken. When she met David, her words proved that. "It is entirely my fault, Sir," she said. "I didn't see the messengers you sent."[13] In other words she was saying, "If I had seen them, I would have used my influence to prevent this trouble."

Abigail's attitude was both tactful and impressive. Although she truthfully called her husband a bad-tempered fool, she identified with him in acknowledging fault. In her attitude and resultant actions, she followed the same principle other great people in God's kingdom would follow.

Think about a difficult situation you are currently facing. What would it look like to speak the truth with tact and humility in that situation?

Nehemiah[14] and Daniel,[15] for example, would later identify with the guilt of the Jewish people who were disobedient to God. Abigail asked no forgiveness for Nabal; she only requested it for herself.

Abigail's attitude, as well as her words, impressed David. As soon as the two groups met on the trail and Abigail saw David, she quickly dismounted. She bowed low before him out of respect. The future king of Israel and a servant of God who had been ignored by her husband as an unworthy person

-----

[13] 1 Samuel 25:25, author's paraphrase
[14] Nehemiah 1:4-11
[15] Daniel 9:3-19

now received her honor. The men on whom Nabal didn't want to waste water received wine offered to them by his wife.

How can you show honor and respect to someone dishonored by the world?

Solomon later remarked that a gift makes room for a person and brings him in the presence of great men.[16] Abigail experienced that lesson. The presents she sent ahead had softened David's heart and cooled off his fury. Her appearance and her words now could do the rest.

Consider the concept of softening someone's heart before approaching a difficult conversation. How might you apply that in your life?

What she continued to say showed such exceptional wisdom and insight that it can best be described with what James later in the New Testament called the "wisdom that comes from heaven." Such wisdom is "first of all pure; then peace-loving, considerate, submissive, full of mercy and good fruit, impartial and sincere."[17]

The most impressive thing about Abigail was that she did not exhibit a false front. She was seen as she really was. The

[16] Proverbs 18:16
[17] James 3:17

circumstances had not allowed her time to reflect thoroughly about the situation beforehand. There had been no time to gather strength, courage, or wisdom. There had been no time for intellectual or spiritual bravado. The storms of life blow away all but who we truly are, and immediate reactions then become the garb in which we are seen.

This was Abigail's attitude toward the holy God. Her heart trembled before Him. She loved Him above everything else and was convinced that above all else a human being had to consider Him. Nobody, she knew, should try to deceive Him. He could not be deceived, and the consequences of such an attempt would be painful.

Does your attitude toward God inform your identity? If you tend to put up false fronts with people, why do you think you do that? How might you live more authentically?

God had blessed David abundantly. Suddenly, as she faced him, Abigail saw that the blessings David had already experienced would be small compared to what the Lord was still planning to do for the future king.

From her deep respect for God, Abigail had gleaned a love for His servant, for this fellow human being. Her love was pure, sincere, and spontaneous. Through her reliance on

God, Abigail also maintained a proper attitude toward herself. Instead of being self-centered, she was modest and avoided self-pity.

Solomon has much to say about becoming wise (Proverbs 1:7; 2:1-6; 9:10). What are the steps necessary to acquire wisdom?

Although tactfully trying to save the lives of Nabal and his men, she seemed to be driven by a deeper motive. She was thinking about those who in this situation were threatened by desire for revenge. In blind fury, David and his men were about to commit a sin that they would always regret. The crime he was about to commit would be irreparable. A heavy weight would burden his conscience the rest of his days. The stain of blood from both the innocent and the guilty would be on his hands.

Abigail reminded David of the favor of God that he was enjoying, the special protection he was experiencing. She drew his attention to the privileged future awaiting him under the blessed hand of God as Israel's future king. David's name was connected with the name of God. Through his rejection of David, Nabal had dishonored God's name. But the future king was also on the brink of putting an indelible disgrace on that name. In a quick-tempered thirst for blood, he was willing to take his rights into his own hands and kill innocent people.

Abigail was convinced that God would punish Nabal for his impertinence toward His anointed one. But she knew that God did not need David to execute judgment. She didn't reprove David. She only painted the consequences of his rash decision, beginning her plea with the words, "As the LORD your God lives."[18] She did this with such natural eloquence that the poet David found it hard not to be fascinated by her style of delivery.

Do you intervene when you see other God followers about to step into sin? How should Abigail's actions and perspective inform your response in such a situation?

Abigail was God-centered. She put God first in her thoughts and exemplified Him in everything she said. Her plea, therefore, was based on what was best for David and not on her own interests. Her motivating force was love for David as a fellow human being.

What Abigail was hoping for happened. David's conscience awakened. Her appeal based on God's character and sovereign power disarmed him. "Praise be to the LORD, the God of Israel, who has sent you today to meet me," David exclaimed. "May you be blessed for your good judgment and for keeping me from bloodshed this day and from

---
[18] 1 Samuel 25:26

avenging myself with my own hands. Otherwise, as surely as the LORD, the God of Israel, lives, who has kept me from harming you, if you had not come quickly to meet me, not one male belonging to Nabal would have been left alive by daybreak."[19]

With these words, David thanked the woman who had watched over his conscience and kept him from sin and remorse. Because of her direct spiritual approach to the problem, he discovered how clouded his own view was and how self-centered he had been because of his personal involvement. David then reestablished a proper sight on God, who through this woman had kept him from making a terrible mistake.

Abigail, who fully realized the extent and the far-reaching results of David's plan, had acted with wisdom and insight. She not only prevented a man from becoming a murderer, but saved the reputation of a future king. David, a man so highly respected that future generations would refer to Jesus Christ as "the Son of David," did not lose his self-respect. He conquered his anger and through self-control won a greater victory than the control of a city.[20] Most important of all, however, was the fact that David didn't sin against the Lord. He did not give God a reason to sorrow. God's enemies did not get a chance to slander His holy name. "Go home in peace. I have heard your words and granted your request."[21] Those were his parting words to Abigail.

[19] 1 Samuel 25:32-34
[20] Proverbs 16:32
[21] 1 Samuel 25:35

*Have any of your actions given God's
enemies a chance to slander His name?
How might you approach decisions in
the future from that perspective?*

Abigail had viewed the situation correctly. Things did turn out badly for Nabal. When he heard from his wife the next morning what had happened the previous day, his reaction of fury and fright resulted in a stroke. He died ten days later, experiencing in his body the lesson that no one can scoff at God and remain unpunished.

When David heard that Nabal had died, he praised and thanked God for paying Nabal back.[22] God had kept him from taking matters into his own hands. David then showed what an unforgettable impression Abigail had made on him. Right away, without wasting a minute, he asked her to become his wife. Abigail gladly agreed.

Abigail's petition, "When the LORD your God has brought my lord success, remember your servant,"[23] received surprising fulfillment. She knew from experience the loneliness of a marriage in which the partners had little in common. But she now became the wife of a man with whom she shared many things: courage, faithfulness, an active intellect, and discretionary insight.

David and Abigail's greatest unity, however, lay in their

[22] 1 Samuel 25:39
[23] 1 Samuel 25:31

attitudes toward God. He had first place in both their hearts. Abigail experienced how God could work all things together for good for those who love Him.[24] She had unexpectedly become a wife of the king of Israel.

Through Abigail's keen insight and wise approach to a difficult situation, David received the opportunity to remain before God as he was, the man after God's own heart. He was still able to fulfill the purpose for which he and every human being had been created: to bring honor to the name of God.[25] As the future king, he would have missed that chance completely had not a woman come into his life at the right time and watched over his conscience, thus preventing him from insulting God.

Abigail used wisdom to show tremendous leadership in the midst of a leadership void. Do you view wisdom as a key piece of your leadership? How are you cultivating wisdom in your life?

---

[24] Romans 8:28
[25] Revelation 4:9-11; 5:11-14

4
THE QUEEN OF SHEBA

A Woman Who Desired to Be Wiser

Since the day before yesterday I have been called to a task so heavy that no one who even for a moment considers the weight thereof should desire it, but also so wonderful that all I can say is, who am I that I am privileged to do this.

QUEEN JULIANA OF THE NETHERLANDS, IN HER ADDRESS WHEN ASCENDING THE THRONE, SEPTEMBER 6, 1948

READ

1 Kings 10:1-10, 13; Matthew 12:42

• • •

SLOWLY, THE LONG CARAVAN CREPT ALONG the ascending road from Jericho to Jerusalem. The heavily loaded camels carried their burdens with nodding heads. The men tending them drove them onward, knowing that the end of the long trip was in sight.

The woman in the center of the party wondered if the exertion of this strenuous journey she had planned would be rewarded. It had taken weeks to cover more than two thousand miles. The cold nights and scorchingly hot days had seemed endless. The countryside had been as sunbaked and unpleasant as a moonscape. Worst of all were the lashing sandstorms and raging winds of the wilderness.

But in her heart she knew she must go. At home in her royal palace in Sheba, she had heard repeatedly about Solomon, the king of Israel, the man who appeared to be immensely rich and unbelievably wise. His fame was known throughout the East and "the whole world sought audience with Solomon to hear the wisdom God had put in his heart."[1] Many kings visited and consulted with him. They honored him with rich gifts.[2]

She had many questions—about her personal life, about her royal obligations, about God.

Who in your network of relationships displays exceptional wisdom and leadership? What can you learn from that person?

The remarkable thing about the rumors she had heard about Solomon was that they were always connected with the name of the Lord. Yahweh, the God of Israel, was said to be the source of Solomon's prosperity. She knew many gods herself—gods of the sea, and of the land, of war, of wine, of day and of night, but they had never given a solution to any problem. Would this One be able to do that?

The way the queen ordered her priorities proves she was a

[1] 1 Kings 10:24
[2] 2 Chronicles 9:22-24

wise woman. In her wisdom, she accepted the limitations of her own knowledge and insight. She wanted to know more and was willing to make many sacrifices in order to gain wisdom. Her time, money, and effort were spent in attaining this goal.

---

*What are your limitations in your areas
of leadership (whether in the home,
in relationships, at church, etc.)?
Who might help you fill those gaps?*

True wisdom goes hand in hand with humility. The queen of Sheba was humble enough to tell the outside world that she was searching for more and that she was not satisfied with her state. Anyone who saw the passing caravan knew that the queen of Sheba was en route to Jerusalem to consult the wise Solomon.

As she came around the last bend in the road, she saw the city of Jerusalem situated on the mountains. Some of the dominant buildings drew her attention, particularly the palace of the king and the temple of his God. Behind her trudged the camels, bent under their costly burdens of rare spices, gold, and precious stones, the value of which could not even be guessed. (One estimate of a hundred and twenty talents of gold would be worth about 151 million dollars today.)

Solomon, the tenth son of David and the second of his union with Bathsheba, was the third king of Israel. He was also called by the prophet Nathan and according to God's will by the name *Jedidiah*, which means, "loved by God."[3]

After Solomon had inherited the throne from his father, God had appeared to him in a dream one night and asked him, "What shall I give you?" The reply of the young man showed his humility and dependence: "Give your servant a discerning heart to govern your people and to distinguish between right and wrong. For who is able to govern this great people of yours?"[4] The answer was so well pleasing in the sight of God that He added riches and honor to wisdom so great that it would never be equaled. Solomon rose head and shoulders above all other kings. His people experienced a golden era in their history.

What is something you have recently asked of God? What were your motivations in making that request?

At this time in history, Egypt, Assyria, and Babylon were weak. The great days of Homer's Greece were yet ahead. Israel was the mightiest kingdom in the world. Jerusalem was the most beautiful city. No building could compare in beauty with the temple. In this setting, one monarch went to visit another. It was not a state visit, but one of a private nature.

[3] 2 Samuel 12:24-25
[4] 1 Kings 3:9

The conversation was stimulating. The queen was humble enough to reveal her hunger for wisdom. She asked Solomon many questions. Solomon, she found, was an open man— a person with seemingly infinite understanding. Like her, he also filled the high but lonely role of a ruler. Consequently, he was someone who could understand her fully. He himself had wrestled with the same problems.

Who in your life is a kindred spirit, dealing with similar circumstances and struggles? What have you learned from that person?

To her amazement and admiration there was no question too deep or too involved for him. He had an answer for everything. She saw that he truly was blessed by God. He had not only intellectual wisdom but common-sense knowledge that was applicable in practical, daily situations. She saw this in the way his house had been built, in the manners of his servants and ministers, in the quality of his meals, and in the variety of the drinks. Every detail of his life was permeated with wisdom. Also, his faith in God affected every aspect of his life. It was pure. It was real. It was the center of his existence.

King Solomon not only involved her in his daily duties but also shared with her about how he served God. And there she discovered the true secret of his successful life. When Solomon offered his sacrifices to God, he identified himself with the innocent animal that was being slaughtered in his place, for his sin.[5] This revealed a seed of truth to the queen of Sheba.

———————

What truth has emerged in your life through the example or words of someone of wisdom? How have you acted on that truth?

———————

Solomon's life was freed because his sins were forgiven; this fact was based on God's appointed means. The shed blood of an innocent creature guaranteed that he—the guilty one—could exist in full freedom.[6] His fellowship with God was the source of all his wisdom, his understanding,[7] and his prosperity.[8]

Solomon's aim in life, she discovered, was not to learn and teach wisdom, but to fear God. Solomon kept His commandments and declared emphatically that this was what God desired of all men, including kings.[9]

The queen was amazed. She was without words. Her highest expectations had been exceeded. "I didn't believe what I heard about your wisdom," she said. "It seemed too omnipotent. But the truth greatly surpassed all rumors. I hadn't heard half of it."[10]

The queen envied the people who served this king, the

[5] Leviticus 1:1-9; 9:7
[6] Leviticus 17:11
[7] Proverbs 2:6; 9:10
[8] Proverbs 10:22
[9] Ecclesiastes 12:9-13
[10] 1 Kings 10:7, author's paraphrase

subjects over whom he had authority. She acknowledged that wisdom was to be preferred above all else.[11] Most remarkably, she stated that Solomon was a love gift from God to His people, so that they might be ruled well.

What would it look like for you to be a gift from God to the people around you?

Her meeting with King Solomon had enriched her mentally and materially. The king shared graciously with her not only his vast understanding, but riches far beyond the precious gifts she had brought him.[12] The worth of the most valued gift she received could not be given a monetary figure. For it was the knowledge she gained about God, who is the source of true wisdom.[13]

The queen of Sheba was a woman who made history. Even Jesus Christ cited her as an example. He praised her for sparing no cost or trouble to hear the wisdom of Solomon. By that action she condemned those who don't take wisdom seriously. She provides a splendid example of the importance of subjecting the things of God to a closer investigation. And she provided proof of her deep insight when she accepted the opportunity to learn from someone else—someone who was wiser than she.[14] She didn't just listen to the rumors that

[11] Proverbs 8:11
[12] 2 Chronicles 9:12
[13] Ecclesiastes 2:26
[14] Ephesians 5:16

Solomon was a wise man. She did everything possible to seek
him out to discover the source of his wisdom.[15]

But was her only enrichment intellectual? Was that her
sole satisfaction? Or did her heart stretch out to God Himself,
the Source of wisdom,[16] the God with whom even Solomon
could not be compared? For the greatest wisdom comes not
from the mind, but from the heart. The hope of such a man
shall not be cut off.[17]

---

*What does purely human wisdom look like?
How does it differ from godly wisdom? What
form does wisdom typically take in your life?*

Was the queen truly wise? Did she fully understand all
Solomon told her? Did she apply the wisdom she saw in
Solomon? Was her heart changed? Did she fulfill the objec-
tives of the plan she had set out to accomplish?[18] Completely?

Her search was a failure if she did not find God. Then
she would be a tragic figure, instead of the perfect example
she is. The Bible does not answer these questions directly.
But perhaps the answer can be found in Jesus' words when
He put her above the Jews, using her as an example to some
Pharisees and scribes of His time. Isn't this proof that she
learned her lessons? The queen of Sheba was a woman who
spared no cost or trouble to become wiser.

[15] Proverbs 2:1-6
[16] Isaiah 11:2; 2 Corinthians 1:30
[17] Proverbs 24:14
[18] 2 Corinthians 8:10-11

5

HULDAH

A Woman Who Helped Lead an Apostate Nation Back to God

Prophecy (Heb. nebu'ah) in the Bible does not concern itself primarily with foretelling future events, in the sense in which one speaks of a weather prophet or a financial forecaster. It deals rather with forthtelling the intuitively felt will of God for a specific situation in the life of an individual or a nation.

FROM *HARPER'S BIBLE DICTIONARY*

READ

2 Chronicles 34; 35:1-19

. . .

ACCORDING TO THE LAW OF MOSES, the Israelites could count on God's exceptional blessing and prosperity because they were His own exalted people. He had chosen them above all other nations.[1]

But God had given His people a measuring stick to live by: His commandments. To enable His people to obey Him, He had carefully described those laws. His people were not left in the dark concerning what He expected from them. They knew exactly what He required.

God told them to hide the laws in their hearts, to teach

---

[1] Deuteronomy 7:6

their children the Word of God, and to allow thoughts of Him to permeate their personal lives and those of their families. All their activities were to be influenced by God's leading.[2]

Obeying the Word of God, therefore, would not be too difficult for the Israelites. Obedience to Him did not lie outside their reach or above their strength. On the contrary, they had heard His laws from childhood and carried them in their hearts, ready to recite them at a moment's notice.[3] All God expected from them was their willingness to live according to His directions. They would do this with His help, through His power. In that way the whole world would be able to see the happiness of a nation that walked with God.

A heart of true obedience springs out of depth of relationship with God. What in your life is God asking you to surrender to Him in obedience?

The privileges of being God's chosen people, however, were tied to one condition: They had to remain faithful to Him. If they failed to be faithful, the results would be terrifying. If they rejected God, He would reject them.[4] Unforeseen catastrophes would befall them, and in the end they would not remain in the land that God, through Moses, had promised them.[5]

---

[2] Deuteronomy 6:6-9
[3] Deuteronomy 30:14
[4] Hosea 4:6
[5] Deuteronomy 28:1-64

At the beginning, especially as long as the Israelites were led by good kings, everything went smoothly. During the reign of David, who had stayed passionately true to Yahweh, God had blessed Israel. During the reign of David's son Solomon, who had been loved for his piety and wisdom, the fame of Israel spread.

Since that time, however, the Israelites had gradually degenerated spiritually. More and more, they had departed from their covenant with God. Few of the previous Israelite kings had turned as far away from God as Manasseh and Amon, the grandfather and father of King Josiah. Few other kings had been so wicked, so backsliding. None had served the idols so repulsively.[6]

Enter the prophetess Huldah. She lived in a time when the Israelite people had left God. They no longer obeyed His Word. The nation had become apostate, following the letter of the law but turning away from the heart of God's intent.

Although her name meant "weasel," Huldah fortunately did not allow that to affect her character. Her life did not in any way resemble that shy, marten-like little animal. During Huldah's time, people were needed who would dare to speak up for their convictions undauntedly, who were not afraid to act.

Do you feel trapped by the perceptions of others?
How have you let other people define you?

---

[6] 2 Chronicles 33:1-25

Huldah served as a mouthpiece for God. Her special calling did not place her outside society, for she was a housewife at the same time. She was the wife of Shallum, the man in charge of King Josiah's wardrobe. Huldah cared for her husband daily, but her marriage didn't stand in the way of her calling. She combined one responsibility with the other.

8 yrs old - ruled for 31 yrs. Song David

What responsibilities do you have? What service for the Kingdom might God be calling you to combine with your current responsibilities?

Huldah held court not far from the temple buildings. There, at her post in the new part of Jerusalem, she daily gave the people advice concerning the Lord. Despite Israel's backslidden condition, there were still a few people who inquired after God.

Huldah carried on her duties openly, without being hindered. She did not need to hide herself as other prophets had been forced to do. For the first time in many years, Judah had a king who served God. King Josiah, following in the steps of his illustrious forefather David, carefully obeyed the laws of God and did not depart from them. Undoubtedly, his dedication to God was the result of his mother Jedidah's influence. He began to cleanse the land of idols, tearing down the altars of the false gods and grinding the idols into powder. He also hired workers to repair and improve the temple of God.[7]

[7] 2 Chronicles 34:1-13

In her court, Huldah grew accustomed to the noises of the repairmen. Then one afternoon, she saw five men approaching her. She easily recognized Hilkiah, the high priest, and Shaphan, the secretary, and several other servants of the king. Their faces were serious, their speech measured.

"We have special orders from his majesty the king," stated Hilkiah. "It concerns the Law of Moses. I found it in the house of God while we were bringing out the money that we needed for the repair work."[8]

"We have read it to the king," Shaphan continued. "He is frightened because we as a nation have not kept the written Law God has given. His majesty has torn his clothes. He is ashamed about the sin of his people. He understands that the situation is very serious, for he fears the wrath of God."[9]

It was soon clear to Huldah that the men had come to her to discover God's will concerning this newly found book. If she asked herself why the king had consulted her instead of the prophet Jeremiah, who lived during the same time, she didn't show it. Like other prophetesses in the past—Miriam[10] and Deborah[11]—Huldah was used to working with men, calmly and with dignity.

God needed a human being who could speak His Word on earth. In that ancient culture, He typically used men, but this particular time He used a woman.

Huldah rightly understood that she should not try to place herself above those seeking her help. Neither did she try

[8] 2 Chronicles 34:14-15, author's paraphrase
[9] 2 Chronicles 34:18-21, author's paraphrase
[10] Exodus 15:20
[11] Judges 4:4

to escape her responsibilities because she didn't feel capable.
God was looking for someone who could function as His
instrument.

---

*Do you ever opt out of doing something God
has asked of you because you feel inadequate?
What might you learn from Huldah about
responding from a place of weakness?*

Jehovah be praised, Huldah thought. *Josiah will not treat
the Book of the Law like an antiquity and put it away in a col-
lection. He understands that God's Book cannot be treated like
an ornament in the royal library. The Law is there to be applied.*

Huldah's answer was clear, without reserve. She showed
no respect of persons, for it was God Himself who spoke
through her lips, challenging the people.

"Thus says the LORD, the God of Israel, 'Tell the man
who sent you to me, thus says the LORD . . .'" Those four
words—"thus says the LORD"—proved the credibility of her
words as a prophetess.[12]

---

*When you offer advice or insight, do you
turn to Scripture? How might Scripture lend
more weight and credibility to your words?*

---

[12] 2 Chronicles 34:23-24, NASB

Huldah then predicted the national downfall of the people. They had treated God's Word carelessly and become apostate, serving idols instead of the living God. Hers was a terrible message of doom,[13] but Huldah held nothing back. She was not afraid of the consequences these words might have for her personally.

What does it look like to treat God's Word carelessly in our modern context? Have you ever been guilty of this?

Yet God's words did not simply contain judgment; they spoke of grace as well. God had noticed the love and faithfulness Josiah was showing toward Him, his sensitive response to Scripture. So He postponed His judgment till after Josiah's death.[14] Then under King Zedekiah, judgment would be executed over the people. At that time the cup of God's wrath would be full to the brim. Reparation would no longer be possible, because Israel had not responded to God's repeated calls for conversion.[15] The nation had ignored His summons: "O land, land, land, hear the word of the LORD!"[16] Jerusalem and the temple would be destroyed and the people forced into exile.[17]

After the messengers delivered Huldah's strong message

---

[13] 2 Chronicles 34:24-25
[14] 2 Chronicles 34:26-28
[15] Jeremiah 29:19
[16] Jeremiah 22:29
[17] 2 Chronicles 36:15-21

to the king, there was no doubt in his mind that God had spoken through her. It was also evident to him that immediate action had to be taken.

Right away he went to the temple with the leaders of the people and read the Law of God to all the inhabitants of Jerusalem and Judah, both small and great.[18]

The people listened attentively. Like the king, they were convinced that God had spoken through the prophetess Huldah. Consequently a revival started among the people that had never been seen before. The king, the leaders, and the entire nation made a new covenant with God. Together they solemnly pledged that from that point on they would serve the Lord. They were willing to obey His Word with all their hearts and souls.

A thorough reformation resulted. The cleansing from idols was carefully continued, and moral boundaries were set. This cleansing was not restricted to the capital city. The entire country—from northern Geba to southern Beersheba— became involved.[19] Most important of all, the Passover was celebrated again. The Israelites had forgotten how God had delivered them in the past. They had ignored the sacrifice that pointed to the coming Christ. They had forgotten the commemoration of the exodus from Egypt, an event that God through Moses had instituted to be an annual observance.[20] For many years they had not celebrated this feast.

Josiah continued to live up to the norm that God had set

[18] 2 Chronicles 34:30
[19] 2 Kings 23:4-8
[20] Exodus 12:1-17; 23:14-15

for a king: "When he takes the throne of his kingdom, he is to write for himself on a scroll a copy of this law, taken from that of the Levitical priests. It is to be with him, and he is to read it all the days of his life so that he may learn to revere the LORD his God and follow carefully all the words of this law and these decrees."[21]

Why do you study God's Word? How often do you spend time in Scripture?

After Josiah's meditation and application of God's Word, he experienced God's blessing, a truth that many other scrolls had described.[22] As certain as disobedience was followed by God's curse, so obedience was always followed by His blessing.

Listening to the words of Scripture changed not only King Josiah's life but the entire nation, which experienced the most thorough reformation of worship Judah had ever known. An apostate nation returned to its living God.

The final judgment of God could not be averted, however. Too many generations of Israelites had sinned too heavily. But the people who lived during the time of the prophetess Huldah did receive a number of years' respite.

Although Huldah's name only briefly lightened up history, the influence of her life was far-reaching. The destiny

[21] Deuteronomy 17:18-19
[22] Joshua 1:8; Psalm 1:1-3

of an entire nation shifted because she coupled her name with the Word of God. Huldah knew that Word. Therefore she could freely exhort and encourage other people with it.

Huldah disclosed no secrets of a far future, unlike other prophets and prophetesses. She occupied herself with the task of revealing God's will through a medium that He had used for centuries. She applied His will to the special situation of the Israelite nation and its individual people. She helped them rediscover lost truths. When her people once again gave their attention to the Word of God—listening to it, reading it, studying it, meditating on it—marvelous things began to happen. When human beings are willing to do what God expects of them, things happen that no one had ever thought possible.

Modern-day prophets call people back to the truths of God's Word in powerful and compelling ways. What modern-day prophets do you see around you?

Huldah, like many other women, was a housewife. But her commitment to the Word of God and her courage to ally herself strongly with it distinguished her from most of her countrymen. When the great opportunity in her life arose, she was prepared.

6

THE SHUNAMMITE

A Woman Who Was a Creative Thinker

Did [Elisha] ever look through his windows down the next twenty-eight centuries, and contemplate what multiplicities of comfort to 'prophets' yet unborn would during that time develop from his aboriginal bed, table, stool and candlestick?

THERON BROWN, QUOTED IN HERBERT LOCKYER,
THE WOMEN OF THE BIBLE

READ

2 Kings 4:8-37

• • •

WITH A FEW STRONG LINES, the Bible draws her portrait—a great woman, very rich, married to an older man, childless. Her name is not mentioned. She was called the Shunammite after the name of her city.

Shunem was situated a little north of Jezreel near Nain, a city that became well known nearly nine hundred years later because Jesus raised a widow's son from death there.

In her marriage, the Shunammite was no drudge who could only give her assent, displaying no personal initiative. She was younger than her husband and more energetic. She offered ideas but only carried them out after discussing them with him. She shared her plans with him, and decision making was a joint effort.

Mature people don't desire to dominate their marriage. Instead, they seek to work harmoniously together so that the marriage can function according to God's will. This can take place even when other factors, such as a great difference in age, are not particularly favorable. God creates each human being uniquely. It is up to each individual—husband and wife—to realize what his or her gifts are and to use those gifts to their full potential.

What people in your life use their gifts to complement the gifts of others? How do they do so? In what ways can you model your actions off of their example?

The Shunammite woman was extremely rich and could easily have allowed herself to become undisciplined, enjoying all the things money could buy. Being a childless woman with an older husband, she could have easily led a dried-up life without purpose, nursing self-pity. But she didn't.

In what ways are you tempted to slide into an easier way of living? What would be the consequences of giving in to such a temptation?

This woman had a wealth of interest in the world around her. She thought of others first, not of herself. She watched her environment attentively and had noticed among the many who passed her house daily that one individual was exceptional. Being hospitable, she invited him to a meal, for she realized that he was, indeed, an unusual person. He was the prophet Elisha.

While she, as a housewife, took care of her daily responsibilities, she asked herself the question, *What can I do for this servant of God?* She received what was, certainly for her time, an original idea—*I'll make a guest room for him! Not a temporal, tent-like thing, but something that is solid and will last.* With her husband's help, she built a guest room for Elisha on the upper level of the house.[1]

How can you encourage and serve the servants of God (pastors, ministry leaders, missionaries) that you know?

The Shunammite, in desiring to serve God, received a creative idea from Him. She created something new, something usable for His service.

There was a bed, table, stool, and lampstand in the room. She made it a room where Elisha could work as well as sleep. She didn't forget anything.

[1] 2 Kings 14:8-10

So Elisha stayed with them. Everything had been arranged for prolonged and repeated usage. Undoubtedly, there was also room for his servant Gehazi. She enjoyed using her money to support the Lord's prophet. Instead of offering money so Elisha could secure lodging and food for himself, she took the trouble to build brand-new quarters for him. In sharing her possessions, she gave of herself. As a result, God rewarded her.

Elisha had asked her through his servant Gehazi, "Since you have taken all this trouble for us, what can we do for you?"

The grateful woman had replied that she had no request for she had everything she needed. The observant Gehazi later pointed out to his master, "She has no son, and her husband is old."[2]

But when she had received the promise that she would bear a son, she didn't dare believe it. "No, my lord, O man of God; please do not lie to your maidservant."[3] But it had not been a deception. It was real. A godly reality! A year later she gave birth to a son.

One day when the little boy was about three or four years old, he accompanied his father to the fields. There he became ill and died within a few hours. His mother put his dead body on the bed of the prophet in the room where he prayed and meditated. She saw only one possible solution—God!

Since God had given her this son, He was the only One who could help. She rushed to His representative, Elisha, who was then at Carmel. Had her thoughts wandered back to that other prophet, Elijah, who had also raised a child

[2] 2 Kings 4:13-14, author's paraphrase
[3] 2 Kings 4:15

from the dead, the child of the widow of Zarephath? Didn't his spirit rest upon Elisha?

Read Psalm 77. What past works of God in your life give you increased faith for the future?

There was no time to waste. Though she informed her husband she was going to visit the prophet, she didn't waste time with further explanations. Had a distance of twenty-five miles ever seemed so long before? *Is it sensible of me to make this trip*, she asked herself, *since my son is dead already?*

Elisha could see from a distance that something was wrong. He wanted to send his servant Gehazi back with her to help. But she was not satisfied with that. She told Elisha she would return only if he himself would go with her. Before having her son, she had been satisfied with her situation in life. She hadn't asked Elisha for a son, but now she missed her child dearly. She felt that the only one who could help her was the man who was instrumental in helping her get the child from God. Since she had totally dedicated herself to meeting Elisha's needs, she now expected him to return with her. Elisha was persuaded and went with her.

When they arrived at her home, Elisha, just as Elijah had before him, stretched himself over the tiny corpse and raised him from death. The Shunammite then received her son for the second time. First she had received him at birth; now she received him from the dead. She did not need to make funeral preparations, so she prepared for a feast!

This was not the only blessing bestowed upon the Shunammite. When the country was threatened by a famine some years later, she was warned by the prophet in time to move away with her family and escape starvation. Not until seven years later did she return to her country. During her absence she had lost her home and fields. She asked the king to restore these to her. Not only did he do that, but he also gave her all of its fruits![4]

Why? Because she was the woman whose son Elisha had restored to life and because of her contribution to him and the Kingdom of God.

The Shunammite was a woman who thought creatively. A woman who, by her unselfish dedication to someone else, opened the floodgates of blessing upon herself. The person who gives becomes the one who receives. This is always true for a person who trusts in God.[5]

Have you cultivated a pattern of giving in your life? How has God blessed your faithfulness? (Remember—blessing is not necessarily material!)

Creativity comes from the Latin word *creatus* and is related to the word *creator*. It was the Shunammite woman's relationship with God, the Creator, that made her what she was.

[4] 2 Kings 8:1-6
[5] Luke 6:38

A genuine walk with God leads to creativity. The person who asks how she can serve God with what she has receives ideas, so to speak, straight from heaven. These are not emotional or presumptuous ideas, but practical and usable ones within the framework of the potential God gives to each person. God's Holy Spirit inspires creativity.

What role does creativity play in your places of leadership? What is one thing you can do this week to combine your creative and leadership gifts?

For the Shunammite this did not mean laboring directly for the temple of God, like Bezalel and Oholiab, the designers of the tabernacle.[6] Instead, she served God within her own home. By doing so she scratched away the label of "routine" from the occupation of "housewife." She used her material possessions for the well-being of others, and God blessed her.

---

[6] Exodus 31:1-11

7
ESTHER

A Queen Who Risked Her Life for Her People

Trust is not a passive state of mind. It is a vigorous act of the soul by which we choose to lay hold on the promises of God and cling to them despite the adversity that at times seeks to overwhelm us.

JERRY BRIDGES, *TRUSTING GOD*

READ

Esther 4:1, 5-16; Esther 7:1-6; Esther 8:15-17

• • •

THE STORY OF QUEEN ESTHER IS REMARKABLE. It has the fairy-tale atmosphere of Scheherazade's 1,001 nights mixed with the scorching smell of Hitler's gas chambers. And while the name of God doesn't appear once in the book of Esther, His presence is evident on every page.

Esther appeared on the scene after another woman, Queen Vashti, had disappeared behind the royal backdrop. Esther was the wife of the immensely rich Persian king, Xerxes, who ruled over 127 provinces from India to Ethiopia from 486 BC to 465 BC. His winter palace was in Susa, nearly two hundred miles east of Babylon. It had floors and pillars of marble, hung with white, green, and blue curtains that were held back with cords of fine linen. The royal family and their guests reclined on couches of gold and silver. During feasts they drank from vessels of gold, no two of which were alike.

Esther, a beautiful young woman with a disposition to match, had won the hearts of the royal household. She was not a Persian, but a Jewish orphan who had been raised by her cousin Mordecai, an exile from Jerusalem who served the royal court. He cared for her as her father would have, and she obeyed him like a daughter, even though she was the queen.

The king's chancellor, Haman, an Amalekite, hated Mordecai. Haman was brilliant, ambitious, and rude. He spared no one. However, the king respected him highly and ordered all servants at the royal court to bow down before him. Mordecai was the only person who refused to do this. Because he was a Jew, the only person he would bow before was God. Haman was so embittered by this rejection that he decided to kill Mordecai and all other Jews in the great Persian Empire.

He conceived a scheme so subtle and watertight that no Jew would be able to escape. All would be caught in the net he was spreading. The total annihilation of the Jews—God's people—was announced. The king's signature had made it possible for Haman to wipe them off the globe forever. Royal couriers took the fastest animals and rushed to every corner of the immense empire to announce the coming calamity. The Jews were appalled and terrified.

Esther had been married to Xerxes for five years. At the request of Mordecai, she had remained silent about her Jewish heritage, but he kept her informed daily of the situation. With the grim extinction of the Jews in sight, Mordecai felt that the only solution was for Esther to intervene.

"Go to your husband the king and ask for his help to save your people," he ordered Esther.[1] Your people! That meant she must reveal her Jewish origins. How would the king react? Would he feel she had deceived him? Did he hate her race as Haman and many others hated it?

There was another obstacle. No one was allowed to go before the king without being summoned—not even the queen. To do so would mean risking her life. She had no guarantee that he still loved her as before. Maybe another woman had taken her place.

She told Mordecai that she hadn't been called to the king for thirty days. But Mordecai was relentless, telling her that she was the only one who could intervene. "Don't think for a moment that because you're in the palace you will escape when all other Jews are killed," he said. "If you keep quiet at a time like this, deliverance and relief for the Jews will arise from some other place, but you and your relatives will die. Who knows if perhaps you were made queen for just such a time as this?"[2]

"From some other place. . . ." Mordecai was thinking about God. God would not allow this impudent murder of the Jewish nation. Throughout the ages He had promised

[1] Esther 4:6-8, author's paraphrase
[2] Esther 4:12-14, NLT

that the Messiah would come through this people. Haman could not prevent this. Neither could Satan. Though the need for deliverance was immediate, Mordecai's trust in God was solid.

What is the foundation for your trust in God?
How does this impact your view of trials?

The future of God's people had seldom hung on such a thin thread. But God's counterattack was ready. He did not execute it by a supernatural intervention. No miracle of nature,[3] no angel,[4] would save His people. Instead, a young woman would. Would this plan succeed? Would the queen cooperate with God's plan, or would she fail?

"God is looking for an instrument, Esther, a human being. Are you willing to give your life? He placed you in this strategic position long before, for He knew of the coming catastrophe. God's solution is you."[5]

In what areas of your life might God be
asking you to act as His solution? What
things might be holding you back?

Esther didn't receive God's message through the imposing words of an established prophet. She received no heavenly

[3] Exodus 14:21-30
[4] Numbers 20:16
[5] Esther 4:14, author's paraphrase

vision. She was led by the words of a relative. God's leading could not have been more inauspicious. Yet she accepted Mordecai's words as the words of God.

———

Have you ever experienced God providing leading through the words of someone in your life? What did you learn from that situation?

———

Young Esther, who had always presented a mild manner, now proved that she was made of the fiber of heroes. This crisis situation revealed the power of her life: God. She was willing to subject her life to His plans. She desired to do His will. "Call all the Jews in Susa together," she said, "and let them fast with me and my maids for three days and three nights."[6]

———

Consider Esther's call to fasting in light of Isaiah 58:3-7, Zechariah 7:4-7, and Matthew 6:16-18. What can you learn from this?

———

She was now publicly identifying herself with her people. Her call to fasting was a call to prayer.[7] She realized she was powerless and had no help to offer. Help could only come from the Lord, the God of Israel. Therefore, she planned to assail His heavenly throne with prayer for three days and nights. Esther

———

[6] Esther 4:16, author's paraphrase
[7] Ezra 8:23; Daniel 9:3

was deeply aware of her need for God's guidance. She wanted assurance that He had appointed the requested task. She knew that God revealed Himself in answer to prayer, and she needed wisdom and courage to act properly. Whom should she ask for advice except the One who was the Source of all wisdom and who distributed it in answer to prayer?

Despite the weight Mordecai's perspective carried, Esther still intentionally went before God for guidance. Do you make prayer the most important part of your decision-making process? If not, how might you intentionally develop a pattern of prayer in every situation?

"Then in spite of the law, I will go to the king. And if I die, I die."[8] She had burned her bridges behind her. This young woman was willing to risk her position, her life, and her future for her people.

After the days of prayer, Esther groomed herself meticulously and went to the king, who was apparently taken up with the affairs of the kingdom. When he saw Esther, his heart was touched. He held out his golden scepter to her as proof that her life was safe. He asked, "What is your request, Queen Esther? It will be granted to you."

The first part of her prayer had been answered. Her life was spared. And God had set ajar the door of salvation for

---

[8] Esther 4:16, author's paraphrase

her people. She had not prayed for wisdom in vain, however. She sensed that this was neither the time nor the place
for her urgent request. Her insight into this situation reveals
that she was a wise woman in control of her emotions and
one who didn't need to make hasty decisions. She was also a
woman who realized very practically that the way to a man's
heart is often through his stomach. She invited the king to a
meal—along with Haman.

*Have you ever made a decision out
of emotion? How do you think that was
reflected in the outcome of your decision?*

During that meal the king asked her again, "What is your
request? I will grant it to you." Esther moved carefully, step
by step, waiting upon God. In her heart she felt that she still
needed to gain time. It was not yet God's time. "Come back
together tomorrow," she requested.[9] And that proved to be
God's leading.

That night the king could not sleep. A courtier read to
him from the book of the chronicles of his people. Important
facts that had been in the dark came into the open. They
fit into the jigsaw puzzle of God's plan. Recently Mordecai
had revealed a conspiracy against the king and, thus, saved
the king's life. But Mordecai had never been rewarded. This
negligence must be corrected, the king decided. And Haman,

[9] Esther 5:6-7, author's paraphrase

the man who had erected an eighty-three-foot high gallows near his house with the intention of hanging Mordecai, was ordered to reward him.

The following day during the meal, Esther revealed her request. Touchingly, she pleaded with the king for the lives of her people. And for her own life: "If we had only been sold into slavery, I would have held my tongue," she said.[10]

But it was not just the lives of the Jews that hung in the balance; the well-being of the king was also at stake. A consequence far worse than losing his servants and far worse than the chain-reaction of hatred against him would occur—he would be turning against God. God had called this people the apple of His eye,[11] and He would protect and keep them. No one could harm this race without risking His wrath.[12] Not even a king. Therefore, Esther wanted to protect him. Her insight and approach demanded the king's respect.

Godly leadership includes pointing people toward God's perspective. What are specific ways you can do this in your life?

Esther succeeded in convincing the king. "Who is the man and where is he who would presume in his heart to do such a thing?" was the king's startling response. Esther's finger

[10] Esther 7:4, author's paraphrase
[11] Deuteronomy 32:10
[12] Zechariah 2:8-9

pointed to Haman, his fellow guest and most outstanding sub- ject. "That wicked man there—Haman," she replied.[13]

Then everything came to light. The gallows that had been erected near Haman's house waited for the execution of Mordecai, but the king changed this plan. "Hang Haman on it," the king commanded.[14] It was done.

Haman's wife and his wise friends had been right. They had told him, "If this Mordecai is a Jew, you cannot pre- vail against him. On the contrary, you will surely fall before him."[15] It would have been wise if Haman had learned from the history of his ancestors, the Amalekites. God was against them because they were against His people.[16] Haman found that hatred is a very dangerous emotion, one that usually turns against the one who unleashes it.

Esther had saved not only her life but also the lives of her people. The New Testament says that Christians should shine like lights in this world, like bright stars in the night.[17] Esther was such a star—which is precisely the meaning of her name.

What does it look like to shine like a light in the world? In what ways could you increase the effectiveness of your light?

The words of her husband to annihilate the Jews were so mighty that they could not simply be withdrawn. A

[13] Esther 7:5-6, author's paraphrase
[14] Esther 7:9 NASB
[15] Esther 6:13, author's paraphrase
[16] Exodus 17:8-16; Deuteronomy 25:17-19
[17] Philippians 2:15

contradictory order was necessary. "Write whatever pleases you concerning the Jews," the king said to her. "I will sign it and seal it with my ring."[18]

The heroine who had saved the Jews by risking her own life received the privilege of telling them this wonderful news! Instead of being a woman behind the scenes, she had become someone of importance. Her words would weigh heavily from then on.

Faithfulness wherever God places us increases our effectiveness. Do you lead behind the scenes or out in front? How effective do you feel your leadership is?

The good news arrived before the date of the mass slaughter. God saw to that. The day Haman had marked on the calendar to be a day of sorrow was one of joy. Many non-Jews became Jews because they were so deeply impressed by what had happened. They wanted to be on the side of the Lord.

The day of gladness became a day of commemoration. The feast of Purim was instituted. At this feast even today, Jews all over the world remember what Queen Esther did for them. Every year when Purim is celebrated, the Jews read the book of Esther. She is highly respected. The Talmud even seems to prefer this book above the Psalms and the Prophets.

[18] Esther 8:8 author's paraphrase

Thirty years later Nehemiah would rebuild the walls of Jerusalem. Without Queen Esther this would have been impossible. It is difficult to imagine the course of history without her. Humanly speaking, if there had been no Esther, there would be no Jewish nation. And without the nation, there would not have been a Messiah. And without the Messiah, the world would be lost.

The Bible is full of people whose decision to follow God in their brief moment in history helped point the way for Jesus. How is your life a part of this bigger picture?

Unbeknownst to her, Esther paved the way for the coming Christ. Through her, God has also indicated that His guidance is available to His followers for making decisions. These decisions should be based upon the Word of God,[19] tested by prayer[20] and the counsel of others,[21] and dependent upon an inner assurance[22] and God-opened doors.[23]

[19] Luke 11:28
[20] James 1:5
[21] Proverbs 15:22
[22] 1 John 3:21
[23] Revelation 3:7-8

8

MARY OF BETHANY

A Woman Who Did What She Could

Friendship with God is reserved for those who reverence him.
With them alone he shares the secrets of his promises.

PSALM 25:14, TLB

READ

John 12:1-11

• • •

NO ONE PAID MUCH ATTENTION TO HER when she entered
the room. She glanced at the men there and then seated herself behind the guest of honor. With a simple motion, she
arranged her long dress and felt for the little jar still hidden
between its pleats. Her entrance had not disturbed the conversation of the guests. The deep voices of the men continued
to fill the room. She was accustomed to sitting at the feet of
Jesus, and those present had seen her do this before.[1]

While the men ate and talked, Mary's thoughts went back
to the first time that Jesus and His disciples had come to her
home. He had brought about a radical change in her, as He

---
[1] Luke 10:39

alone could do. She didn't recognize her own life anymore. *He started by giving us His friendship*, she mused. That was an unknown experience. Up until that time, a wide gulf had existed between men and women. Jewish men thanked God every morning in their prayers that He had not created them as a slave, a heathen, or a woman.

Do you view your relationship with Jesus as a friendship? What elements of a friendship define how you relate to Him?

It had been apparent immediately that He was different. His concern was not just for a man or just for a woman. He was interested in the total human being, man or woman.[2]

He had introduced a new respect for women. He had offered her possibilities that had been unknown until then. He had lifted her to His plan. That was why she had felt so entirely at ease in His presence. Without any shyness, she had come and sat down in the midst of the men who were listening to His words.

Jesus values you and calls you worthy. Do you feel at ease in His presence? How should His perspective of you inform how you relate to others?

---

[2] Galatians 3:28

As she sat at His feet and listened to Him, there was a hunger in her heart, a thirst after God. The purpose of her existence had become clear in listening to this man. A conviction grew within her: "I am created for God. I exist because of Him."[3]

This gave meaning and color to her life. It revealed previously undreamed of opportunities. She lived her life in the fellowship of Christ.[4] This was the purpose of life to which she felt called. The first result was a hunger for His Word. Bread—food for the body alone—cannot satisfy a human being. The inner person must be fed with the Word of God.[5]

In times when you have not engaged consistently with the Word of God, what has been different in your attitude and outlook?

While she satisfied her thirst with His words and as her knowledge about Him increased, her feelings matured into a decision: "I shall do for Him what I can." Gratitude swelled in her heart. She watched the men talking for a moment longer. Then she was distracted by Martha, who waited upon the Lord and the other men. *Martha*, she thought, *how much He has done for you! So very much.* Martha had an active, outgoing personality. Her love for the Lord revealed itself in her service for Him because she was a woman who thought and

[3] Revelation 4:11
[4] 1 Corinthians 1:9
[5] Matthew 4:4

acted quickly. She was the opposite of Mary, who was more introspective and quiet by nature. It was encouraging to see how the Lord understood both of them. He loved each one according to her own character.

The outworking of our relationship with the Lord reflects the uniqueness of our inner connection with Him. How does your character express itself in how you serve God and relate to Him?

From Martha, Mary's eyes wandered to Lazarus, the host, who was sitting next to the Master. She could not help feasting her eyes upon her brother. He had come back from the dead. He lived! She would never forget the moment when Jesus had raised His voice and shouted, "Lazarus, come out!"[6]

There was also some shame in her heart when she remembered that occasion. She and Martha had wondered why the Master hadn't come more quickly. They could not understand His delay, which had been almost more painful than the loss of their brother. Never before in their lives had they felt so deserted. Looking back they could see how shortsighted they had been. Later, they had understood why Christ had acted this way. He had done it entirely for His

Father's will, for Lazarus's resurrection had honored God. Many people were moved to believe.

To honor God and provide salvation for His people—that was Jesus' aim. This proved to be hard for Jesus, for the fiery hatred of the Jewish leaders, which had only been smoldering prior to that time, now was stirred up into a flame that would destroy Him. In snatching Lazarus away from death, He had signed His own death sentence.

In six days it would be Passover.

Did this thought suddenly open her eyes? Did she feel instinctively that Jesus had come today to say farewell? He was also preparing for the festivities at hand. This Passover, the animal blood shed at the Temple to redeem the sins of the people would not be the only blood shed.[7] In Jerusalem a greater sacrifice would be offered. Jesus would die.

She remembered all the times He had spoken of His sufferings to come.[8] There remained no question in her mind: Jesus would have to die. He was the Lamb of God who would take away not merely the sin of a single nation, but of the entire world.[9]

Much had become clear to Mary during her friendship with Jesus as she saturated herself with His words. She had developed a spiritual insight and understanding of things that other people didn't see.

In the Word of God, faith and deeds inseparably belong together. Mary felt this in the depths of her soul. She felt a

[7] Exodus 12:13, 21-28
[8] Mark 8:31
[9] John 1:29

stirring desire to do something. She wanted to express her thankfulness to her Lord, perhaps for the last time. Her hands moved along her robe. They touched the little jar hidden there. Her decision was made.

The perfume was very costly. The amount in the jar represented a laborer's wages for an entire year.[10] Nard was an embalming oil. *This belongs at a funeral*, she thought. *No!* She suppressed this thought as quickly as it came to her mind. It was the living Lord who must receive her worship, not the dead. It was time to do something for Him now.

Reflect on Mary's sacrifice. What might you be able to offer out of gratitude to the Lord?

She quickly carried out her plan as if she were afraid someone would keep her from doing it—as if there were not much time left.

The sweet-smelling drops of perfume pouring out upon Jesus' feet were an expression of Mary's gratitude. Without holding back, she poured out her soul. Her homage was without words. How could simple words express her many thoughts? Sometimes it is easier to convey one's deepest thoughts by a look or motion rather than words.

Her surroundings were completely forgotten, as she was taken up with her thoughts about the Lord. Lovingly, she dried His feet with her hair. Suddenly the room was silent.

[10] John 12:5

The talking had stopped. The thick perfumed odor had pervaded the room—it had placed her squarely in the center of attention. What had she done?

---

*In what ways can your actions and
perspectives lead others to worship Jesus?
What might you do to bring glory to
Him and call others to do the same?*

What to the Master was a sweet smell was offensive to the nostrils of Judas Iscariot. His criticism was biting: "Why wasn't this perfume sold and the money given to the poor?"[11] Others supported him. Although Judas sounded altruistic, his interest in the poor was a pretense. He would rather have put the cash in the moneybag he carried so that he could help himself.

---

*Have you ever been criticized for something
you did to glorify God? How did you respond?*

Again, Mary's good intentions were interpreted the wrong way, like the time she had been accused of laziness by her sister.[12] Jesus knew her motives, however. He had also defended her on that occasion. Now He said, "Leave her alone. Why are you bothering her? She has done a beautiful thing to me."[13]

[11] John 12:5, author's paraphrase
[12] Luke 10:40-41
[13] Mark 14:6

Mary was the only one who realized His time on earth was drawing to an end. Anything she could do for Him was more important than anything else.

He not only defended her, but He praised her: "She did what she could."[14]

What have you been equipped to do to show your love for God? Don't compare your gifts and opportunities to those of anyone else. God has crafted you for specific purposes and positioned you in a specific place. What might cause God to say, "She did what she could"?

Quietly listening to His words had helped Mary grow into a woman with spiritual insight. She had become a woman who understood the secrets of God. She knew precisely what to do and when.

The Master's words not only revealed Mary's thoughts but also clarified the way God looks at things. His highest praise is reserved for the person who is interested in His Word and who acts upon it. Such a person doesn't need to fear criticism from others. She doesn't need to withdraw when people nag at her. Such a person has the best advocate available: Jesus Himself.

---

[14] Mark 14:8

9

MARY MAGDALENE

A Woman Who Led the Way in Following Christ

Run, Mary! lift thy heavenly voice;
Cry, cry, and heed not how;
Make all the new-risen world rejoice—
Its first apostle thou!

GEORGE MACDONALD, "MARY MAGDALENE"

READ

John 20:1-18; Mark 16:9

• • •

MAGDALA WAS SITUATED at the northwestern shore of the Sea of Galilee, about three miles from the well-known city of Capernaum. There Mary met Jesus for the first time. There He delivered her from Satan, who through his demons had taken possession of her. There the miracle of her life had taken place, the full extent of which she could only understand gradually.

Until that meeting Mary Magdalene had been a pitiable woman. She only understood how much she was to be pitied when she saw other possessed people. They could no longer fit into normal society. Almost more animal than human, they roved about in caves—lunatic men and women with distorted faces and wild eyes. Though they had been created by God, they were now strangled by Satan.

Sin no longer has power over us, but in our weakness we often don't take hold of the truth that God has set us free. Do you ever feel as though you are being strangled by Satan? What are specific things you can do to cling to truth?

After Jesus commanded the seven demons to leave Mary, everything about her changed. Her bound spirit became free; her cramped limbs were now relaxed. The glance of her eyes became as calm as the surface of the nearby sea on a quiet day.

Mary would never be able to express exactly what had happened to her. The experience was too great to tell. Only one person understood it completely: Jesus. So she refused to leave Him after her healing. She left Magdala—a thriving place of industry—and went with Him.

Mary Magdalene wanted to stay close to Jesus for many reasons. First, she knew by experience that she could not afford to minimize the power of Satan. Unless she stayed close to the Lord—who was superior to the devil—she alone would have no defense against Satan's attacks. She had to prevent the evil one from possessing her again. If that should happen, her end would be worse than before.[1]

How do you stay close to Jesus? Describe a time when your closeness to Him served as a clear defense against Satan's attacks.

Although Mary stayed close to Christ to protect herself, it was not her only reason. She also followed Him out of love and gratitude. She wanted to do more than just give Him her possessions and stay at home, telling the people of Magdala what had happened to her.

Mary Magdalene, who once was possessed by the devil, now had received another passion. Jesus Christ had taken hold of her. He had turned her "from darkness to light, and from the power of Satan to God"[2]—literally.

That change would affect her entire future life. From that moment on, Mary would acknowledge only one Lord. She chose to follow Him, whatever the cost, till the end. Thus she accompanied Jesus and His disciples, as did other women who had also been healed of demonic possession.[3]

Does your life serve as a visible testament of Christ's work? How might you more clearly show the world that He has changed you?

---

[1] Luke 11:24-26
[2] Acts 26:18
[3] Luke 8:1-3

• • •

It was early morning, three days after Jesus had been cru-
cified. The streets were quiet. The sun was not up yet.
Darkness enveloped the narrow streets of Jerusalem, but
Mary Magdalene hardly noticed. Neither was she aware of the
other women around her: Salome, Joanna, Mary the mother
of James and Joseph, and some others.[4] As a group, they were
on their way to the grave of Jesus to finish embalming His
body. They had stopped their work Friday night because the
Sabbath observance had begun.[5]

They walked rapidly toward the Place of the Skull, located
just outside the city, and made good progress. The merchants,
who in a few hours would make the narrow streets even nar-
rower with their displays of goods, had not yet arrived. The
beggars, who would ask for alms with outstretched hands
and starry eyes, were still asleep.

Mary Magdalene walked in front of the little group. She
was not interested in what was happening around her. Her
thoughts ran only one way, departing and arriving at the
same point: the Master.

---

*What might it look like for your thoughts
to depart and arrive with Jesus? How often
is Jesus present in your thoughts?*

---

[4] Luke 24:10; Mark 16:1
[5] John 19:31

Over and over again, her thoughts flashed back to the events of the past days. During the trip from Galilee to Jerusalem, the disciples and the other women who were with Jesus had felt heavy-hearted. Jesus had told them what would be awaiting Him.

Despite His prediction, their entry into Jerusalem had been festive. Great crowds had enthusiastically met them, overwhelmed with joy. "Hosanna to the Son of David," they had shouted. "Blessed is he who comes in the name of the Lord! Hosanna in the highest heaven!"[6] While uttering these shouts of joy, many had taken off their coats and spread them on the road before Jesus. Others cut branches from the palm trees and did the same with them.[7]

The ecstasy did not last long. A few days later, the same inhabitants of Jerusalem cried, "Take him away! Crucify him!"[8]

Mary Magdalene's Master endured intense suffering from that point on. But Mary followed Him faithfully till the end.

She had been present in the judgment building when the crowds demanded His life. She heard Governor Pilate submitting Him to the fury of His enemies. She followed Him when He carried His cross down the street from Pilate's residence toward Calvary, the place where the pronounced judgment was executed. Her heart had shrunk when she saw how the people mocked and scourged her Master, who had shown so much love to them.

Full of sorrow, Mary watched how the scourging wore the

[6] Matthew 21:9
[7] Matthew 21:8
[8] John 19:15

Master out, how He stumbled under the weight of the cross. Like many other people in Jerusalem, she wept as the Master endured horrible torture and walked toward an unjust death. She was powerless to do anything for the One who had done everything for her.

———————————

Read each gospel account of Jesus' crucifixion (Matthew 26-27; Mark 14-15; Luke 22-23; John 18-19). Put yourself in Mary's place. What fears might you have had? What emotions would you feel?

———————————

At the cross, Mary Magdalene and the other women saw the nails driven through His hands and feet. They watched as the soldier drove a spear into His side. Blood and water dripped onto the ground.[9] At that moment her eyes searched in vain for the disciples. All of them except one—John—had deserted their Master.

Extraordinary, terrifying events had followed quickly, one after the other. At midday the sky suddenly turned dark and remained that way for three hours. A strong earthquake broke rocks and opened graves. Many godly men and women who had died came back to life again.[10]

Most terrible of all that was happening was Jesus' cry shortly before His death: "My God, my God, why have you forsaken me?"[11]

———
[9] John 19:34
[10] Matthew 27:45-53
[11] Mark 15:34

Why, she had asked herself, anguished, *does Jesus have to be so forsaken by God and men? Why can't He save Himself? Isn't He powerful? Doesn't He have more power than Satan and death?*

Through her years of following Him, Mary Magdalene had watched Jesus' incredible power over disease, infirmity, and demon possession. Even nature had obeyed His voice. A gusty wind had changed into a peaceful breeze, and white-caps had become a sea of rippling glass.

Why, cried a voice within her, *doesn't He use His power to help Himself? Why?*

Though Jesus' suffering tore at the deepest part of her heart, Mary Magdalene stayed until Jesus whispered, "It is finished."[12] She could not leave the Master who had meant more to her than anybody else.

She watched as He was buried, and afterward, when everyone but Mary the mother of James and Joseph had gone home, Mary Magdalene placed herself near the grave. She didn't leave the gravesite till Jewish law ordered her to do so when the Sabbath began.

But now the Sabbath was over, and while the whole city slept, the women neared the grave. They were relieved; after a day of forced rest they could finally do something. But as they drew closer, questions began to weigh heavily on their minds. "Who will roll the stone away from the entrance of the tomb?" they asked one another.[13] And that was not their only problem.

---

[12] John 19:30
[13] Mark 16:3

Pilate had stationed a guard at the grave and had sealed the stone entrance to keep Jesus' disciples from stealing the body.

The sun was rising as they walked the path to the grave. There was no one else around. They were the first to visit the grave since the day of His death.

Mary caught her breath, then pointed the others toward the entrance of the grave. Were her eyes deceiving her? No, there could be no doubt; the grave lay open. The stone had been rolled away.

Mary Magdalene didn't even look into the tomb—she immediately ran to tell the other disciples what had happened. She was out of breath when she reached the house of Peter and John. "They have taken the Lord out of the tomb," she told them, distressed, "and we don't know where they have put him."[14]

Peter and John returned with Mary. Unlike the women, they did not stay outside the rock-hewn cavern. They stepped inside and discovered that while the body was gone, the grave clothes remained, neatly folded. Thieves would not have done such a thing. Dazed and unsure, the disciples returned to the city.

Mary, however, could not leave the last spot where the body of her Lord had been placed. She remained outside the tomb, tears flowing freely down her cheeks.

Finally, she bent over to look into the tomb—and looked straight into the eyes of angels. Two men in shining white robes were sitting at the place where Jesus' body had

---

[14] John 20:2

lain—one at the head, the other at the feet. "Woman, why are you crying?" they asked her.[15]

"They have taken my Lord away, . . . and I don't know where they have put him," she replied, wiping away her tears with her hand.[16] Then she heard a noise behind her. She turned away from the tomb and saw someone else standing outside. *It is the gardener*, she thought.

"Woman, why are you crying?" the Man asked her.[17] Tears clouded her vision. Without any introduction, she said, "Sir, if you have carried him away, tell me where you have put him, and I will get him."[18]

Mary Magdalene had been faithful to her Lord since her conversion. She had stayed at the cross till the last moment and had been the first at His tomb. Now she wanted to complete her last act of love toward the Master by anointing His body with embalming oil.

Then she heard His voice: "Mary!"[19]

Read each gospel account of the Resurrection (Matthew 28; Mark 16; Luke 24; John 20). Imagine yourself in Mary's place—the depths of despair and confusion . . . and then hearing Jesus speak your name. How does this love make you feel?

----

[15] John 20:13
[16] John 20:13
[17] John 20:15
[18] John 20:15
[19] John 20:16

Only one person ever said her name in that way. No one else spoke it with that same depth, that radiating warmth. A stream of feelings welled up within her—bewilderment, joy, gratitude, and adoration overwhelmed her heart.

"Rabboni!" was what burst from her lips.[20] It was the intimate word for *Master* in homely Aramaic, the language Jesus had used when He talked with her.

At that moment Mary Magdalene became the first witness of Jesus' resurrection. The central truth on which the salvation story hinges was first revealed to her. What a privilege!

The words Jesus spoke proved that, though He was alive again, from that point on things would be different. He prevented her inclination to hold His feet. "Do not hold on to me, for I have not yet ascended to the Father," He said. "Go instead to my brothers and tell them, 'I am ascending to my Father and your Father, to my God and your God.'"[21]

With that commission, the risen Lord also made Mary the first announcer of His resurrection. That honor was not reserved for John, His intimate friend, or Peter, His most prominent disciple. Even Jesus' mother did not enjoy this privilege. It was reserved for Mary Magdalene, the woman who led the way in following Christ.

The story of Mary first of all sheds light on Jesus Christ. It shows His love for a person and His power over Satan. But it also clearly shows the attention He gave to a woman in a time when women were not respected. Her story illustrates the

[20] John 20:16
[21] John 20:17

fact that God does indeed reserve exceptional privileges for those who give themselves out of love and gratitude totally to Him.

What privileges have you been granted because of your relationship with Jesus Christ? How might you share this extraordinary gift with others in your life?

Before Mary met Jesus, her life had been a drab nightmare. After He liberated her from the power of Satan, she began to live a meaningful life. This new life through Christ received an added dimension on the morning of Jesus' resurrection. The earthly relationship with her Master was finished, but a new spiritual one began. Seven weeks later on the Day of Pentecost, the Holy Spirit was given to the believers.[22] Although her name is not mentioned, Mary was certainly among the people present.[23] The Holy Spirit also helped Mary to continue to remain close to Christ. He gave her the power to witness about Him.[24]

Since the time of Mary Magdalene, millions of women have lived, and most of their names have been forgotten. But Mary's continues to live on. May we also be women who love our Master with abandon and, through the depth of our commitment, lead others to follow Him.

[22] Acts 2:1-21
[23] Acts 1:14
[24] Acts 1:8

10
LYDIA

A Businesswoman Who Gave God First Place

No, dear brothers, I am still not all I should be, but I am
bringing all my energies to bear on this one thing: Forgetting
the past and looking forward to what lies ahead, I strain to
reach the end of the race and receive the prize.

PHILIPPIANS 3:13-14, TLB

READ

Acts 16:11-15, 40

• • •

THE SABBATH HAD STARTED IN PHILIPPI.

Philippi was an important city in Macedonia, a center of
commerce between the Aegean and Adriatic Seas. This key
location was the bridge that connected the Middle East to
Europe by means of the Roman highway—the Via Egnatia.

An Asiatic woman walked quickly out of the city to a
spot at the river where a prayer meeting would be held. The
woman, Lydia, was an important person. She directed her
own business. She imported purple cloth, a very costly item
that was worn only by the rich and kings, from her home-
town of Thyatira in Asia Minor.

Lydia was well respected. She lived in a spacious house with many servants. She was a successful businesswoman, for the Lydian purple market was renowned in the Greco-Roman world. Its products were eagerly sought everywhere. Lydia was an intelligent woman, a clear thinker who did her work with enthusiasm and purpose of mind. Her work gave her much contact with interesting people. And being an independent woman at this time in history was an exceptionally interesting occupation.

She did not, like many business people, become totally engrossed in her work. Despite her many obligations, she found time for things of greater importance. She wasn't satisfied, as many of her fellow citizens were, with worshiping Apollo. She worshiped the only true God. She took time out for Him in her busy schedule. Lydia realized that as a businesswoman she needed His guidance, which was why she was on her way to this prayer meeting.

How do you prioritize time with God in the midst of your busy schedule? This is often difficult to do. If you struggle to find the opportunity for intentional time with God each day, pray over possible options for how He might want to open up your schedule. Can you get up earlier? Stay up later? Spend time with Him over your lunch break or while your kids are napping? Commit to making this a priority.

The meeting today was very small and for women only. Apparently there were not ten Jewish men in Philippi—the required number for a synagogue—so instead, the women held an open-air meeting. Today some unexpected guests visited the meeting—educated men. Paul, the great evangelist and missionary apostle, and his companions Silas, Luke, and Timothy had arrived in the city from Troas.

Initially, Paul had had a different plan. He had wanted to go to Bithynia, but the Spirit of Jesus had prevented him in a vision one night. It had been made clear to him that he needed to go to Macedonia.[1] So here he was in Philippi to address these women.

He spoke about the God of Abraham, who had sent His Son to this earth to redeem the people, to bridge the gap that sin had created between God and man. He told them that by faith in Jesus Christ, there was redemption, eternal life, and a new perspective on living.[2] Lydia listened carefully, with all her heart.

Pascal has said that God created a God-shaped vacuum in the human heart that can only be satisfied by God Himself. Lydia was open to the things of God because her heart craved this deeper experience of faith. Lydia's knowledge of God was superficial. She did not know Him as her Father in Jesus Christ. He could reach her heart easily, however, because it was already set on Him and she was sensitive to His Word. It was necessary for her to pay attention to His Word, for while God makes one step toward a person, He then expects the

[1] Acts 16:7-10
[2] Acts 3:13-16; Romans 8:1,16-17

individual to make the next step. God then proves Himself by making the next step.

---

*What steps toward God do you sense
Him asking you to take today?*

The seed of the Word fell into her heart as if onto prepared ground[3] and resulted in a new birth.[4] She found the link that had been missing in her experience—personal faith in Jesus Christ. Lydia had become a Christian. This energetic woman wanted to testify openly about it immediately. She wanted everyone to know of the unspeakable happiness that was now within her. She was baptized. By this she said without words, "I identify myself with the death and resurrection of Jesus Christ, and I am going to begin a new life."[5]

This new convert drew others to Christ like a magnet. And who should be the first to hear but her own household? They listened to the Word and also believed. They, too, confirmed their faith by baptism—and the first church in Philippi was born.

---

*How do you testify about your faith to those
around you? How can you be intentional with
your testimony so that people are exposed
more intentionally to God through you?*

---

[3] Luke 8:15
[4] 1 Peter 1:23
[5] Romans 6:3-5

For Paul, there was no longer any question as to why he had been directed to Macedonia. People were being born again. They were the first Christians in Europe. A new continent was opening for the gospel—through Lydia.

In ages to come, an innumerable throng would follow her example. Like her, they would receive Christ and multiply in following generations. Lydia's enthusiasm for God bore fruit in others' lives. The number of Christians increased through her. This is what God expects all Christians to do. At Creation He commanded humans and beasts to multiply themselves biologically to fill the earth. They were to bear fruit after their kind.[6] When Jesus talked to His disciples about fruit-bearing,[7] He was speaking of people who could spiritually come to life through the seed of His Word.[8] Christians can multiply themselves spiritually by bringing others to Christ. Lydia did this.

Have you multiplied yourself spiritually?
If so, what did this look like? If not,
what is one thing you can do this week
to move toward bearing that fruit?

Being a Christian was a very practical matter for Lydia. She did not become a missionary or a full-time evangelist. She remained in her occupation. She brought credit to her name by submitting herself, her business, and her possessions to maximum service for Christ.

[6] Genesis 1:24-29
[7] John 15:1-16
[8] John 17:20

---

*How can you submit your current
role in life to service for Christ?*

The first thing she submitted was her home. She urged Paul and his companions to stay there. Their acceptance proved they took her faith seriously. In this way she also identified herself with the gospel to the nonbelievers. She was not ashamed of Christ. She was not ashamed even when Paul and Silas, bruised and wounded, returned from prison, where they had been taken illegally. Everyone in the city knew that the distinguished Lydia considered it a privilege to lodge these men.

God desires that Christians open their homes to others and serve one another with what they have received from Him. He desires that they be good managers of the material possessions He has entrusted to them.[9] Those who are hospitable will realize later, to their amazement, that sometimes, unknown to them, they have given angels a place to stay.[10] Abraham and Lot experienced this.[11] Lydia understood this also, though it was not stated in so many words.

---

*What does hospitality look like in your home?
What is one thing you can do this week to
intentionally cultivate godly hospitality?*

---

[9] 1 Peter 4:9-10
[10] Hebrews 13:2
[11] Genesis 18:1-15; 19:1

From then on Lydia's earnings would not be an end in themselves, but a means to further the gospel. Lydia would sell purple cloth to the honor of God. He was at the top of her list of priorities. She was not only in a key position socially but also geographically. The news spread quickly from this commercial city situated on several international travel routes. From then on, not only would bags of purple cloth leave Lydia's home, but the gospel, too, would travel throughout the civilized world.

It is reasonable to assume that a woman who could impress the apostles and her household with her newly founded convictions would be no less successful in convincing her business contacts. Thus, her business was a two-fold success.

---

*What talents and gifts do you use
in your everyday life? How might
you use those talents and gifts more
intentionally for the cause of Christ?*

Some years later when Paul wrote to the Philippian church from his Roman prison, he mentioned the women who worked hard with him to help spread the gospel.[12] He was probably thinking of Lydia and others he met in her home.

Lydia had been given much, and she used it for the Lord.

---
[12] Philippians 1:3-7; 4:3

She is proof of how much God can do through a person who has made Him the first priority in life.

_____

How did Lydia prove that she gave first priority to things of God? What do you learn from her, and how can you work this out in your daily life?

_____

11
PRISCILLA

A Woman Who Preached the Gospel

In the Jewish and Greco-Roman cultures of that time, women were frequently forbidden to read in front of males, let alone to teach them. Apparently, Priscilla had the approval of God, her church, and Apollos to teach theology to a male. Tertullian, a second-century Christian writer and apologist, wrote that "by the holy Prisca the gospel is preached." John Chrysostom called her a teacher of teachers. Other ancient sources also cite the ministry of Priscilla.

HEIDI BRIGHT PARALES, *HIDDEN VOICES*

READ

Acts 18:1-4,18-20,24-26; Romans 16:3-5;
1 Corinthians 16:19

• • •

PRISCILLA. The fact that her name has been preserved in history is proof that she was a remarkable and distinguished woman. The appearance of her name before her husband's is even further proof of this. However respected and interesting her life in Rome might have been, it came to an abrupt end in AD 50 when the emperor Claudius expelled all Jews from that city.

Priscilla and Aquila left Rome and headed toward Asia Minor, finally settling in Corinth.

It appeared as if their lives had reached a dead end, but God's blueprint for them would soon reveal an exciting new beginning. A fascinating new life of service was awaiting them.

Think of a time in your life when you felt as though you had reached a dead end. What new work did God do following that time? Do you find encouragement in God's past faithfulness in the midst of trials? How does this help you encourage others? (See 2 Corinthians 1:3-4.)

They had left much behind—their possessions and their friends. But they were a harmonious couple, and their marriage was still intact. They had no need of the warning that Paul later made to the loose-living Corinthians: "Do not be yoked together with unbelievers. For what do righteousness and wickedness have in common? Or what fellowship can light have with darkness?"[1] This couple had become one in a special way, as they walked together in their faith.[2]

They had arrived in Corinth just before Paul. He had confidence in this couple and was willing to invest his life in them in order that the gospel could be spread further.

---

[1] 2 Corinthians 6:14
[2] Amos 3:3

Both Priscilla and Aquila had learned an occupation. Even rich Jews saw to it that their children learned a trade. And hadn't Jesus of Nazareth, the carpenter, indeed proved that working with one's hands was an honorable thing?

They were tentmakers, and this trade proved to be a link between them and Paul, for he was also a tentmaker. They not only worked together but also lived together. Paul knew well that the best kind of training he could give came from being together day after day. Like Jesus, he selected his future coworkers carefully.[3]

Who are your coworkers in faith?
Who is someone in your life you can
invest in as a future coworker?

They worked in a small outdoor shop, similar to the ones common in the Middle East today. They talked a lot as, day after day, goatskins and hides changed under their fingers into useful tent coverings. Each day Paul tailored the Word of God to their needs. And they learned how to apply it.[4]

Priscilla and her husband listened eagerly to Paul's teachings. They were interested in the message that Paul preached at the synagogue on the Sabbath. They prayed for him. And when he experienced problems, they were with him, prepared to give their lives for him. Priscilla and Aquila were

[3] Mark 3:14
[4] Philippians 4:9

united not only by their faith and the same trade, but also in their respect and friendship for Paul. This loyalty must have meant much to this lonely man, for shortly before his death, he sent them his greetings.[5]

Read Acts 28:30-31. What in both this passage and Priscilla's life proved to be a unique opportunity to further the gospel?

Priscilla, who watched the smallest details of Paul's life, was as much impressed by what he did as by what he said. He made it very clear how one could follow Christ.[6]

As orthodox Jews, Priscilla and Aquila knew the Old Testament teachings well. But the new knowledge of a faith in Christ and the working of an indwelling Holy Spirit in the human heart were truths that gave them new dimensions in living.

Paul left Corinth after eighteen months, during which a church had been formed. Priscilla and Aquila accompanied him to Ephesus. Though the believing Jews there fervently desired him to stay, he left shortly after his arrival. He was on the move again—this time to Caesarea.

The fruit of the time Paul had spent with Priscilla and Aquila now became evident. He was no longer needed in Ephesus because they could stay there and capably replace him. His life work was being continued through them.

[5] 2 Timothy 4:19
[6] 1 Corinthians 11:1

Who has invested in your spiritual walk? What legacy has that person imparted to you?

This became very clear when Apollos, a gifted Jewish preacher from Alexandria, arrived in Ephesus. He spoke to the people about Jesus with glowing and convincing words. What he preached was true but incomplete. Priscilla and Aquila immediately detected where his message fell short. They realized that his preaching stopped with the work of John the Baptist. He didn't know the wonderful gospel story—the results of the death and resurrection of Christ. He seemed to have never heard about the outpouring of the Holy Spirit.

Showing no condescension, they tactfully invited him into their home where, very personally, they explained the full gospel to him. The Bible describes this in just a few words, but the part and character of Priscilla cannot be hidden.

What is the foundation for correcting misunderstandings of the Bible? With what attitude should you correct those who teach an incomplete gospel?

She spoke with such love and tact that the learned and gifted preacher eagerly accepted the words of the lay couple.

That was the striking thing about Priscilla: Though she had a strong personality, she offered her leadership humbly.

How does your personality inform
your leadership style? What can you
learn from Priscilla's example?

Was this why those with whom she colabored appreciated her? What did Apollos hear from Priscilla and her husband? Precisely what Paul had told them. They proved to Apollos by the Scriptures that Jesus was the promised Messiah, the Christ.

Priscilla and Aquila had started a spiritual chain reaction similar to the one Paul later wrote about to Timothy, his spiritual son: "And the things you have heard me say in the presence of many witnesses entrust to reliable people who will also be qualified to teach others."[7]

What Paul had taught Priscilla—or Prisca as he liked to call her—and Aquila, they had in turn passed on to Apollos. He also began passing it on to others—to the people of Corinth! Thus, Priscilla and Aquila multiplied themselves. They began to bear spiritual fruit. They touched a life, and that life blossomed into a disciple,[8] whom they knew they could trust to preach the true and complete gospel to others also. So while Paul traveled to Palestine before returning to

----

[7] 2 Timothy 2:2
[8] 1 Corinthians 16:12

Asia Minor, and while Priscilla and Aquila opened their home in Ephesus to build the church, Apollos fed the Christians in Corinth. God's Word grew rapidly because the seed of the Word[9] fell into prepared ground. Personal follow-up caused growth and new life.

Discipleship is an intentional action to which Jesus calls all Christians. Are you discipling someone? If not, with whom can you develop a discipleship relationship? How would you go about entering that discipleship relationship?

After some time the couple was no longer needed in Ephesus. A church had been established there that could continue their work. God called them back to Rome. Claudius was dead. Once again the home of Priscilla and Aquila became the meeting place for Christians, this time in Rome.

Paul now called them his fellow-workers in Jesus Christ. The former pupils had grown into valued colaborers. They were remembered gratefully in all the churches by the Jews and non-Jews alike.

Their stay in Rome was short, probably because of the gruesome persecution of Christians under Nero. But they were there long enough to begin another church. Wherever they went, lives were changed and renewed as people came to believe in Jesus Christ.

---

[9] 1 Peter 1:23

How do you impact your environment? What legacy of faith do you want to leave?

They returned to Ephesus. Tradition has it that Priscilla and Aquila finally died as martyrs—beheaded. The Roman Catholic Church commemorates their names on July 8 in the history of the martyrs.

Priscilla was a remarkable woman and wife. She received a prominent place in history because of her friendship and colaborship with Paul.

History and inscriptions more often mention her name than that of her husband. Was she more famous than her husband because she was more intelligent, better educated, or stronger of character? Or was she perhaps a Christian before him? Perhaps she led him to Christ?[10] The Bible doesn't say.

Her marriage is fascinating, however. These partners functioned harmoniously together in all aspects of life—in their faith, in their social and spiritual interests, in their friendships, in the place God's Word played in their lives—both for their personal study and preaching—and in their willingness to give themselves to others without restriction. They honored the relationship that God desires to see between Himself and the marriage partners.[11] Their purpose in life was to give themselves totally to God.

[10] 1 Peter 3:1-2
[11] 1 Corinthians 11:3

---

*Marriage as God intended is a dynamic
partnership for His kingdom, as we see in
the marriage of Priscilla and Aquila. Where
do you see this modeled in your community?
What can you learn from those models?*

Life requested much from Priscilla. She had to have great vitality to adapt again and again to new situations. She made long and tiring trips. She risked her life to further the gospel. She was exceptional for that period of history because she worked with men as an equal, yet won their love and respect.

Priscilla's life also indicates possibilities that have long been neglected—opening one's home for both evangelism and building of the church. Did Paul learn this from Priscilla and Aquila? For he used this very means in the future, when all other doors had been closed to him.[12] Even today Priscilla inspires many to make their homes available for the expansion of the kingdom of God.

Much more important than Priscilla's name in history is the fact that through the ages she has stimulated people to follow Christ—in more than one way. Ages after her death, her life reveals to women today the secrets of a fruitful life and of a marriage that is useful in proclaiming the gospel.

---

[12] Acts 28:30-31

12
PHOEBE

A Single Woman with a Heart of Servant Leadership

In country after country some of the most attractive people
I meet are single missionaries. They are absolutely the most
life-affirming people anywhere. They obviously channel their
creative drive and energies to help others around them in
Jesus' name. I watch them and I'm inspired.

ADA LUM, *SINGLE AND HUMAN*

READ

Romans 16:1-2

• • •

PHOEBE, THE SERVANT OF THE CHURCH IN CENCHREA—the
eastern port of Corinth—had finished her journey. It had
been a long and dangerous trip, one that many men hesitated
to make.

Phoebe had traveled over land and over water. Her feet had
blistered from her endless walks over rocky, mountainous roads.
Her nerves had been tested when she crossed from Macedonia
to Italy in a creaky little ship. But under all these circumstances
she always remained conscious of her task. She had to deliver
Paul's letter to the Christians in Rome undamaged.

Finally the contours of the city rose up before her eyes. Rome, the eternal city, lay on its seven hills before her. The Appian Road on which she was walking led into the very heart of the city. For Phoebe, this trip was an exciting adventure in more ways than one.

Through this trip, first of all, her perspective had been extended. It was around AD 57, a time when few people were privileged to travel and most of the travelers were men. It would take centuries before the world—first through the written word and later by means of modern mass media—would be broken open. People still lived in isolation and usually did not know many people outside their own cities.

This trip not only allowed Phoebe to visit another country and one of the most fascinating cities of all times, but also gave her the opportunity to meet other Christians. Apart from sharing the same faith, these Christians differed from her in many ways.

Reflect on a time when you interacted with a Christian from a different context (cultural, socioeconomic, etc.). What did you learn from that interaction?

Phoebe was a single woman, but she was not lonely. Her life was anything but empty. Her fulfillment stemmed from her willingness to serve. By giving of herself to others, Phoebe kept the specter of loneliness at a distance. She knew that living for others draws people, particularly single people, out of their isolation. Being open to meeting the needs of others helped make her life full and rich, an interesting and varied adventure.

Have you ever dealt with loneliness? Did you withdraw from those around you or engage more deeply? Did you consider serving others as an antidote to loneliness? What do you think about that concept?

Phoebe would experience that principle in Rome. The Christians there would not receive her as a stranger. Paul's scroll of parchment, her most precious baggage, contained a warm endorsement for the messenger. So she would be met with cordial interest and would be treated with honor.

"Give her any help she may need," Paul had written.[1] Phoebe, who was always thinking of other people, now would be helped herself. These words witnessed to Paul's loyal friendship and respect for Phoebe.

Paul, who had to postpone his visit to Rome many times,[2] dared to make his first contact with the Roman Christians through Phoebe. It would be three more years before he would be able to visit Rome himself. Until that time, the Roman Church would see him through the eyes of Phoebe.

A prominent Christian leader, Paul put his reputation in the hands of this woman. It was risky for him to become so

---

[1] Romans 16:1-2
[2] Romans 1:13

dependent on another person. With Phoebe, however, Paul dared to take the risk. He knew that she had a good reputation and would represent him. She had proved that she had a heart for God and His service. She was capable and dignified and could be trusted to carry this great responsibility.

What sort of reputation do you have in your community (church, work, friends, family)? Are you the kind of person to whom others would entrust their reputation?

In Paul's letter to the Romans lay his most complete declaration of the gospel. From the city of Rome the message of Christ would spread into the world. In that letter, Paul explained all the basic principles of the gospel. He wanted his readers to know that every human being is a sinner.[3] Every person is born of sinful parents[4] and does sinful deeds, both of which deserve the death penalty. Without any exception, people are lost without God.[5] They are creatures that cannot exist before a holy God.[6] This is indeed the darkest fact of human history.

Paul's letter, however, did not only point to the greatest problem of humanity but also contained God's great solution. Human beings did not need to suffer that terrible punishment. They were not condemned to die for their sin. Each

[3] Romans 3:23
[4] Romans 5:12
[5] Romans 6:23
[6] Romans 3:10-18

person could escape that frightful destiny by appealing to the God-sent Mediator.

Jesus Christ—God's Son—underwent the death penalty even though He was innocent.[7] He gives complete pardon to people who accept His substitutionary work[8] and acknowledge that they are sinners. They must also believe and put their trust in Jesus Christ and publicly declare their decision for Christ.[9]

Those who believe and respond to Christ's message will not be condemned to spiritual death. Instead of being eternally separated from God, they will receive a new, eternal, and spiritual life. They become children of God, and the Holy Spirit will give them a deep inner conviction of this truth.[10]

Continuing to build on the foundation of faith, Paul instructed the Romans about the assurance of salvation.[11] He talked about walking with God and living through the power of the Holy Spirit. These and other great truths Paul defined in the letter that Phoebe, a willing servant of the gospel, was taking to Rome.

Put yourself in the place of those in the Roman church to whom this letter was written. How would you have felt, reading the truths Paul entrusted Phoebe to share, especially in the context of persecution?

---

[7] Romans 5:8
[8] Romans 8:1
[9] Romans 10:9-10
[10] Romans 8:16-17
[11] Romans 8:31-39

The Bible doesn't tell how Phoebe herself came to a personal faith in Christ. The fifty-two words that describe her life are all too few. But her faith was certainly the content of her life and the motivation of her actions. She was a sister in the church where faith in Christ bound all the believers together into one large cross-cultural family. They met one another's needs like brothers and sisters.

Do you consider Christians across the world brothers and sisters? How might you make the cross-cultural nature of our relational faith more of a reality?

With Phoebe, the word *sister* did not merely point to a mutual, spiritual relationship; it also spoke of status. In a society in which the woman was placed far below the man, Phoebe took her place in the large family of the children of God in a completely equal spiritual relationship. From that position she began serving the church.

For Phoebe, serving was not an inferior task. It was not a second-rate fulfillment of life. It became a grand privilege. In the port of Cenchrea, which like every major seaport showed sin in its crudest form, Phoebe's personality radiated light. Was it Phoebe's light? No, the light of Jesus Christ[12] shone through her. Her light was a reflection of His transforming power.

---
[12] John 8:12

We do not know how she helped others. Did she open up her home for the church like Lydia and Priscilla did? Did she offer hospitality to people traveling eastward or westward through the seaport at the Aegean Sea? Or had her help consisted mainly of giving money and goods? These questions have no certain answers. They also are not very important, for we know that Phoebe's services were manifold, sacrificial, and effective.

Phoebe had no husband. She stood in life alone. Yet she was not waiting patiently for someone to relieve her loneliness. She used her solitude to serve others. *Who*, she may have thought, *can do this as unhindered as I? Who can give herself better to others than she who only has to take care of herself?*

That attitude also determined her relationship toward Paul. There is no doubt that to Phoebe, Paul was the great apostle, God's servant. But he was also her "brother." He was a man who also stood alone in life, who needed and appreciated the help of an understanding woman.

Who in your community is standing alone?
How can you encourage and support that person?

Thus it worked out to be an ideal interaction. Whether Phoebe was placed in a special function—that of a deacon, for instance, as we see in some translations—or whether she limited herself to unofficial service, we cannot know for sure.

The first duty could be derived from the term "servant of the church,"[13] the second from the fact that she personally helped Paul and others. But for a woman like Phoebe, this made no difference. She was concerned about things that really mattered—her usefulness to God and other people. Such a servant had little desire for a title. She only wanted to be a human being with a positive influence. She commanded respect because of her faith and vision and because of her total giving of herself to others.

Do you love and serve others out of a desire to glorify God or out of a desire for attention? Have you experienced the blessing of true giving?

Every person needs love and attention. Phoebe was no exception. She received what she needed by first giving her love and talents to others. To use Solomon's words, she was "enriched" because she first gave "freely."[14]

According to the laws of the kingdom of God, when Christians freely give, they receive back abundantly. A person who does not hold back in serving—who joyously and voluntarily spreads love and friendship—will experience God's blessing. "God," Paul writes, "loves a cheerful giver."[15] On such a person He will heap good gifts. Such a person will

[13] Romans 16:1, ESV
[14] Proverbs 11:24-25, ESV
[15] 2 Corinthians 9:7

always have more than enough, in every way; she will have overflowing means to do all kinds of good works.

The question of whether humanity would have a copy of Paul's letter to the Romans if Phoebe had failed is mere speculation. God—the Eternal, the Sovereign, the Almighty One—was not dependent on a human being for the delivery of His message. But the fact remains that He used Phoebe to bring this precious Word of God to the Roman people and to the world.

Paul mentioned Phoebe first in a long list of colaborers, among which eight other women are named.[16] She walked in front of a procession of women who through the ages have served Christ and His church.

---

[16] Romans 16:1-16

About the Author

GIEN KARSSEN was raised in a Christian home and became a Christian at the age of twelve as a result of her parents' lives and training. After she had been married only six weeks, the Nazis interned her husband in a concentration camp, where he died. Just before his death he inscribed Luke 9:62 in his diary: "But Jesus said to him, 'No one, after putting his hand to the plow and looking back, is fit for the kingdom of God'" (NASB). This verse challenged Gien and gave purpose and direction to her life. Using this Scripture as a basis, she found it easier to face difficulties, cancel her own desires, and want God's will only.

She met Dawson Trotman, founder of The Navigators, in 1948 in Doorn, Holland. She started the Navigator ministry there by translating The Navigators' *Topical Memory System* into Dutch and handling all the enrollments. Over the years she worked in many capacities with The Navigators. Women who have been personally helped by Gien Karssen can be found on almost every continent of the globe.

Gien was a popular speaker, Bible study leader, and trainer, as well as a freelance writer for Christian periodicals in Europe. The original edition of *Her Name Is Woman* (Book 1) was her first book and the first book ever published by NavPress. She also wrote *Beside Still Waters* and *The Man Who Was Different*.

Create Intimacy with God

Discover your unique discipleship gifts

The Gentle Art of Discipling Women
978-1-63146-382-2 | $15.99

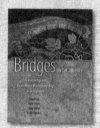

Walk daily with the Lord with conviction and love

Bridges on the Journey
978-1-63146-536-9 | $14.99

Crossroads on the Journey
978-1-63146-537-6 | $14.99

Friends on the Journey
978-1-63146-538-3 | $14.99

Bestselling topical Bible study series for 30 years

Becoming a Woman of Excellence
978-1-63146-564-2 | $9.99

Becoming a Woman of Faith
978-1-61521-021-3 | $9.99

Becoming a Woman of Freedom
978-1-57683-829-7 | $9.99

Becoming a Woman of Grace
978-1-61521-022-0 | $9.99

Becoming a Woman of Prayer
978-1-57683-830-3 | $9.99

Becoming a Woman of Purpose
978-1-57683-831-0 | $9.99

Becoming a Woman of Simplicity
978-1-60006-663-4 | $9.99

Becoming a Woman of Strength
978-1-61521-620-8 | $9.99

Becoming a Woman Who Loves
978-1-61521-023-7 | $9.99

Becoming a Woman Whose God Is Enough
978-1-61291-634-7 | $9.99

Learn from Seasoned Disciplers

Available wherever books are sold.

A NavPress resource published in alliance
with Tyndale House Publishers, Inc.

CP1436

Women of the Bible You Can Relate To

Believers

Jochebed
Hannah
Rahab
The Jewish Maid
Ruth
Mary

Elizabeth
Anna
The Poor Widow
Mary of Jerusalem
Tabitha
Lois and Eunice

Leaders

Miriam
Deborah
Abigail
The Queen of Sheba
Huldah
The Shunammite

Esther
Mary of Bethany
Mary Magdalene
Lydia
Priscilla
Phoebe

Learners

Eve
Sarah
Rebekah
Leah
Dinah
Tamar

Naomi
Bathsheba
The Widow of Zarephath
Martha of Bethany
The Samaritan Woman
Salome

Wanderers

Hagar
Lot's Wife
Rachel
Potiphar's Wife
Delilah
Peninnah

Job's Wife
Orpah
Michal
Jezebel
Herodias
Sapphira

Gien Karssen's vivid storytelling and deep insights will immerse you in the lives of these women. As you grapple with God's role in each woman's life, you will be inspired to live your own life wholeheartedly for God.

The Her Name Is Woman series is a favorite guide for Bible studies and small groups, with relevant Scripture passages and Bible study questions.

Available everywhere books are sold or online at NavPress.com.
1-855-277-9400

CP0927